John Murdoch

The Theosophic Craze

and the great Mahatma Hoax

John Murdoch

The Theosophic Craze
and the great Mahatma Hoax

ISBN/EAN: 9783742867063

Manufactured in Europe, USA, Canada, Australia, Japa

Cover: Foto ©Lupo / pixelio.de

Manufactured and distributed by brebook publishing software (www.brebook.com)

John Murdoch

The Theosophic Craze

THE THEOSOPHIC CRAZE:

ITS HISTORY;

THE GREAT MAHATMA HOAX;

HOW MRS. BESANT WAS BEFOOLED AND DEPOSED;

ITS ATTEMPTED REVIVAL

OF

THE EXPLODED SUPERSTITIONS

OF

THE MIDDLE AGES.

FIRST EDITION, 4,000 COPIES.

𝔐𝔞𝔡𝔯𝔞𝔰:
THE CHRISTIAN LITERATURE SOCIETY.
S. P. C. K. PRESS, VEPERY.

1894.

PREFATORY NOTE.

THE following compilation has been suggested by the visits to India of Mrs. Besant. It brings the history down to the present time.

There is a Latin proverb, *De mortuis nihil nisi bonum,* 'Of the dead let nothing be said but what is good.' Under ordinary circumstances this rule ought to be observed; but when the dead are used to diffuse most pernicious error among millions of the living, the hope of India, the truth ought to be spoken.

Still, it may be said to be unfair to bring charges against the dead who cannot rebut them. They were made in 1884, when Madame Blavatsky was alive, and was publicly challenged to disprove them in a Court of law. (See page 11.)

A careful study of the following papers will show that Madame Blavatsky and her followers are most unsafe religious guides.

The attention of educated Hindus is especially invited to the closing chapters. Instead of accepting what is virtually a godless philosophy, let them hold fast the great truths, that God is our Father in heaven, and that our first duty is to be obedient and loving children. Acknowledging the Fatherhood of God, the Brotherhood of Man follows as a legitimate inference.

J. MURDOCH.

MADRAS, *December, 1894.*

CONTENTS.

	Page
INTRODUCTION	1
SPIRITUALISM	2
COLONEL OLCOTT, "THE PRESIDENT-FOUNDER"	5
MADAME BLAVATSKY, THE REAL FOUNDER	7
THE THEOSOPHICAL SOCIETY IN INDIA	11
EXPLANATION OF MADAME BLAVATSKY'S FRAUDS	17
REPORT OF THE PSYCHICAL RESEARCH SOCIETY	29
MRS. ANNIE BESANT	37
MRS. BESANT'S VISIT TO INDIA	46
HOW MRS. BESANT WAS BEFOOLED	52
MRS. BESANT "DEPOSED BY MASTER'S DIRECTION"	59
THEOSOPHY A RETURN TO EXPLODED SUPERSTITIONS OF THE MIDDLE AGES	60
THE GREAT MAHATMA HOAX	65
MADAME BLAVATSKY'S CONTEMPT FOR HER DUPES	72
"A CORRUPT TREE BRINGETH FORTH EVIL FRUIT"	73
THE STUDY OF HINDUISM	75
SCIENTIFIC STUDIES	76
ANCIENT MONOTHEISM	77
THE TRUE JAGAT GURU, OR WORLD'S TEACHER	79
TESTIMONIES TO CHRISTIANITY	81
A NATIONAL RELIGION	82
NEED OF PRAYER	82
APPENDIX, LIST OF PUBLICATIONS	85

THE THEOSOPHIC CRAZE.

INTRODUCTION.

The following chapters may be fitly introduced by the remarks in *The Times*, when Mrs. Besant gave an address in London on Theosophy:—

"The fact that a large number of persons assembled on Friday in St. James's hall for the purpose of hearing Mrs. Besant discourse upon 'Theosophy,' or, as we presume the words must be translated, upon Divine Wisdom, is surely a curious commentary upon modern claims to intellectual advancement. It was wittily said of a book which once attracted much notice—the 'Vestiges of the Natural History of Creation'—that its publication served to reveal the existence of previously unsuspected strata of ignorance among the classes who were supposed to be educated; and, in like manner, the eagerness with which certain sections of the public join in the pursuit of anything which can excite in them the sensation of wonder may be held to prove that the weighty words in which, nearly forty years ago, Faraday called attention to the almost total absence of any provision for the education of the judgment, are as applicable now as they were to his contemporaries. It probably would not be too much to say that they are still more applicable, or, at least, that they are applicable to a larger proportion of persons; for, in the intervening time, the superficial forms of education have become more and more diffused without any serious attempt to supply the deficiency which Faraday indicated. More people read and marvel; but there is probably no corresponding increase in the number of those who read and think, or who, before they attempt the latter process, address themselves to the work of learning how to accomplish it in a profitable manner. And thus it happens that doctrines and speculations as old as human nature are again and again brought upon the stage, with no other alteration than a change of actors and of costume; and that, as often as they find exponents capable of felicitous expression, or calculated by their own personalities to arouse a feeling of curiosity, they attract audiences to whom their antiquity and their sterility are alike unknown, and who accept words and phrases, which, for the most part, are destitute of intelligible meaning, as if they really conveyed appreciable additions to the sum of contemporary knowledge. The great problems of life, by which all men are daily confronted, such as the unequal distribution of property and other benefits, the origin of evil, and similar questions, have always led to the formation of guesses at truth by speculative philosophers, and these guesses, often times accepted by disciples as revelations, have differed among themselves chiefly to this extent, that each one has been date-marked, so to speak, by the peculiar beliefs, or by the peculiar ignorance, of the time or of the place in which it has its origin. Moreover, the speculators have constantly been acquainted with what may be generically called the phenomena of mediumship; second-sight, mesmerism, hypnotism, and the like; and on the basis of these phenomena they have often claimed, or have been credited with, command of powers of a supernatural order. In a large number of cases, they have also practised the arts of the juggler, and have added what they knew to be deceptions to those tricks of a different kind which, depending upon weakness of the nervous system in those on whom they were performed, the performers may often, in their ignorance, have regarded as being evidence of the possession by themselves of some special gifts or qualities not common to mankind. It is now admitted by all physiologists, that no such interpretation can be correctly placed upon them."—*April* 12, 1891.

1. SPIRITUALISM.

Some account may be fitly given of this system, with which the founders of Theosophy originally started.

Belief in Ghosts.—" Modern Spiritualism," says a writer in the *Encyclopædia Britannica*, " arose from one of the commonest superstitions in the world." Interesting details regarding the different notions entertained of ghosts, or disembodied spirits, will be found in Tylor's *Primitive Culture*. The most troublesome ghosts were supposed to be those of men notorious for their violence during life or of persons who had been murdered.

Faith in ghosts was gradually disappearing among enlightened nations. About seventy years ago, Sir Walter Scott, in his *Demonology and Witchcraft*, could say, "the increasing civilisation of all well-constituted countries has blotted out the belief in apparitions." Their physical causes became understood. Sully says, "Kant observed that the madman is a dreamer awake, and more recently Wundt has remarked that, when asleep, we 'can experience nearly all the phenomena which meet us in lunatic asylums.'"* Some affection of the brain, which in its severer form causes insanity, may, in a milder degree, occasion spectral illusions. The case of Nicolai, a German bookseller, is well known. The following is abridged from his own account :—

"I generally saw human forms of both sexes, but they usually seemed not to take the smallest notice of each other, moving as in a market-place, where all are eager to press through the crowd; at times, however, they seemed to be transacting business with each other. I also saw several times people on horseback, dogs, and birds. I also began to hear them talk : the phantoms sometimes conversed among themselves, but more frequently addressed their discourse to me."†

Nicolai's illusions were caused by too much blood. When some was withdrawn by the application of leeches, the illusions began to fade, and at last they dissolved in the air. Hibbert gives an account of different supposed apparitions, arising from excited states of particular temperaments, &c.

Rise of Spiritualism.—Formerly ghosts, for the most part, moved silently in dim twilight, though noisy apparitions were also known. They likewise contented themselves with terrifying people.

---
* *Illusions*, p. 182. † Hibbert's *Philosophy of Apparitions*, pp. 6, 7.

In 1847-8 they made a new departure, answering questions by means of raps. This first took place in the United States, that land of marvels. Colonel Olcott thus magniloquently describes the new phenomenon :—

"If ever there was a fact of science proved, it is that a new and most mysterious force of *some* kind has been manifesting itself since March 1848, when this mighty modern epiphany was ushered in, with a shower of raps, at an obscure hamlet in New York State. Beginning with these percussive sounds, it has since displayed its energy in a hundred different phenomena, each inexplicable upon any known hypothesis of science, and in almost, if not quite, every country of our globe."*

The "inexplicable phenomena" began with the "so-called 'spirit raps.' By these simple signals the whole modern movement called Spiritualism was ushered in."† Persons supposed to be able to hold intercourse with spirits were called *mediums*. Answers to questions were denoted by a certain number of raps.

The rappings were so successful that the spirits were encouraged to give other manifestations of their presence. Some mediums claimed to have the "power of floating in and moving through the air, of raising tables from the ground and keeping them suspended, and of performing many other supernatural feats."

The first professed mediums were two young sisters of the name of Fox. They were followed by Davis, the "Poughkeepsie Seer," the Eddy Brothers, Katie King, Dr. Slade, and others too numerous to mention.

Spread of Spiritualism.—The believers in this system *claim* to be fifteen millions strong. This is an exaggeration, but they are numerous. "Man," says *The Saturday Review*, "is naturally prone to superstition, and in his earlier stages of culture will invent the strangest theories to account for the phenomena he sees around him. So much of this old leaven is left in us, that any new doctrine, however preposterous it may be, is sure to find adherents."

It was said of the ancient Athenians that they "spent their time in nothing else, but either to tell or to hear some new thing." Spiritualism has been taken up by many in the same way. Some thoughtful men are drawn to it for a higher reason : "Inquirers who live in constant fear that science is trying to demonstrate the truth of materialism, and to rob them of their dearest hope, that of a future life in the society of their departed friends, turn eagerly to what they think ocular evidence of another existence."‡

That there should be so many spiritualists is not surprising. Carlyle, with grim humour, describes the population of the British Islands, about thirty millions, as "mostly fools." Colonel Olcott

---

* *Addresses*, p. 58.   † Ibid, p. 61.   ‡ *Encyclopædia Britannica*, Vol. II.

bears the following testimony to the presence of some of them in India :—

"I can show any of you, if you chose, a bundle of requests for the miraculous cure of physical and mental ailments, the recovery of lost property, and other favours. And, lest my English auditors might be disposed to laugh in their sleeves at Hindu credulity, let me warn them that some of the most preposterous of these requests have come from their own community; some from persons so highly placed that they have asked that their names may be withheld at all hazards." *Addresses*, p. 107.

Reasons for Disbelief in Spiritualism.—The great body of scientific men reject the system for the following reasons :—

1. As a rule these phenomena are exhibited in the presence of 'sensitives,' who are paid for exercising their profession and who prefer to do so in a dark room.
2. As a rule, nothing worth notice has occurred at *séances*,* when competent observers have been present.
3. When strange phenomena have been witnessed, they have often been traced to conscious imposture and *legerdemain*.
4. When conscious imposture does not come in, *unconscious cerebration* and *unconscious muscular action*, supervening on a state of *expectant attention*, are just as deceitful.
5. The received spiritualist theory belongs to the philosophy of savages. A savage looking on at a spiritual *séance* in London would be perfectly at home in the proceedings.
6. The reported doings and sayings of the spirits are trivial, irreverent, useless and shocking.

There is scarcely any literature, not even the records of trials for witchcraft, that is more sad and ludicrous than the accounts of spiritual *séances*.†

Acknowledgments of Trickery.—Mr. Crookes, a noted Spiritualist, makes the following admission :—

"In the countless number of recorded observations I have read, there appear, to be few instances of meetings held for the express purpose of getting the phenomena under test conditions."‡

Colonel Olcott confesses, " a multitude of sickening exposures of the rascality of mediums,...and the average puerility and frequent mendaciousness of the communications received." " Little by little a body of enthusiasts is forming, who would throw a halo of sanctity around the medium, and by doing away with test conditions, invite to the perpetration of gross frauds. Mediums actually caught redhanded in trickery, with their paraphernalia of traps, false panels, wigs and puppets about them, have been able to make their dupes regard them as martyrs to the rage of sceptics, and the damning proofs of their guilt as having been secretly supplied by the unbelievers themselves to strike a blow at their holy cause !§ The voracious credulity of a large body of

---
* Sittings with a view of holding intercourse with spirits.
† Abridged from the *Encyclopædia Britannica*, Vol. II.
‡ Olcott's Lectures, p. 60.
§ These words suggest an application.

Spiritualists has begotten nine-tenths of the dishonest tricks of mediums."*

The foregoing remarks refer only to SPIRITUALISM, properly so called—professed direct intercourse with departed spirits. They do not apply to hypnotism and kindred subjects.

COLONEL OLCOTT.

"THE PRESIDENT-FOUNDER."

Colonel Olcott claims to be the PRESIDENT-FOUNDER of the Theosophical Society. The Supplement to *The Theosophist*, January, 1881, gives an account of his public life as a member of the Bar, as an officer in the Army, Secretary of the National Insurance Convention, Agricultural Editor of *The Tribune*, &c. "Although," he says, "I always took an active part in all that concerned my country and fellow-countrymen, and an especially active one during our late civil war, yet my heart was not set on worldly affairs." Before he met Madame Blavatsky in 1874, he had "ideas that had been the growth of 22 years' experiences, with mediums and circles." He also makes the following candid acknowledgment : "I was in 1874 —a man of clubs, drinking parties, mistresses, a man absorbed in all sorts of worldly public and private undertakings and speculations."†

He acknowledges that he was for 22 years a Spiritualist. His own chief characteristic is the "voracious credulity," with which he charges a "large body" of them. (see page 4).

Colonel Olcott is the author of a remarkable book, *People from the Other World*.‡ In this, in his *Lectures*, and his magazine, *The Theosophist*, he claims to have had the following wonderful experiences :

1. **The acquaintance of fifteen Mahatmas.**—*The Theosophist*, gives the following description of these "great souls :"

"A Mahatma is a personage, who, by special training and education, has evolved those higher faculties and has attained that spiritual knowledge which ordinary humanity will acquire after passing through numberless series of reincarnations during the process of cosmic evolution, provided of course, that they do not go in the meanwhile, against the purposes of Nature, and thus bring on their own annihilation." July, 1884.

Colonel Olcott says in his *Lectures*:

"Within the three years when I was waiting to come to India, I had other visits from the *Mahatmas*, and they were not all Hindus or Cashmiris. I know some fifteen in all, and among them Copts, Tibetans, Chinese, Japanese, Siamese, a Hungarian, and a Cypriote. But whatever they are, however much

---
* Olcott's Lectures, pp. 58, 59, 60.
† *Esoteric Philosophy*, pp. 77, 78.
‡ 8vo. 492 pp. American Publishing Company, 1875.

they may differ externally as to races, religion and caste, they are in perfect agreement as to the fundamentals of occult science, and as to the scientific basis of religion." p. 165.

According to Colonel Olcott, the ancient proficients amongst them, as Zaratushta and Buddha, "knew more about nature than Tyndall does, more about the laws of Force than Balfour Stewart, more about the origin of species than Darwin or Haeckel, more about the human mind and its potentialities than Mandsley or Bain." *Lectures*, p. 149.

2. **The sight of "500 apparitions."**

The President-Founder seems to have been peculiarly favoured in this way. The single Cock-lane ghost in England, during the time of Dr. Johnson, was a wonder for half a century; but Colonel Olcott claims to have seen, from first to last, "more than 500 apparitions of dead persons" at the house of the Eddy Brothers. Among them were:—

"Americans and Europeans, Africans and Asiatics, Red Indians of our Prairies and white people, each wearing his familiar dress, and some even carrying their familiar weapons." *Lectures*, p. 68.

Colonel Olcott's "apparitions" show the wisdom of the course pursued by some nations, both in ancient and modern times, of burying the dress, weapons, &c., of deceased persons with their bodies. How else could the apparitions have been suitably clothed or carried their familiar weapons?

Colonel Olcott had perhaps the unique experience of *weighing spirits*. To do this correctly, he obtained one of Howe's best Standard Platform Scales. His experiments elicited the remarkable fact that the spirits could vary their weight. "Honto," weighed successively 88, 58, 58, and 65 lbs.; "Katie Brink," 77, 59, 52 lbs.*

3. **A sight of the following Marvels:**

1. Showers of roses made to fall in a room.
2. Letters from people in far countries drop from space into my lap.
3. Heard sweet music, coming from afar upon the air, grow louder and louder until it was in the room, and then die away again out in the still atmosphere until it was no more.
4. Writing made to appear upon paper and slates laid upon the floor.
5. Drawings upon the ceiling beyond any one's reach.
6. Pictures upon paper without the employment of pencil or colour.
7. Articles duplicated before my very eyes.
8. A living person instantly disappear before my sight.
9. Jet-black hair cut from a fair haired person's head.
10. Had absent friends and distant scenes shown me in a crystal.
11. In America more than a hundred times, upon opening letters upon various subjects coming to me by the common post from my correspondents in all parts of the world, have found inside, written in their own familiar hand, messages to me from men in India who possess the theosophical knowledge of natural law.

---

* *People from the Other World*, p. 487.

I have not even half exhausted the catalogue of the proofs that have been vouchsafed to me during the last five years as to the reality of Asiatic psychological science. *Lectures*, pp. 73, 74.

MADAME BLAVATSKY.

THE REAL FOUNDER.

EARLY LIFE.

MADAME HELENA PETROVNA BLAVATSKY was born at Ekaterinoslav, in the south of Russia in 1831. Her father was Colonel Peter Hahn. She says, " For over six years, from the time I was eight or nine years old until I grew to the age of fifteen, I had an old spirit who came every night to write through me...In those days this was not called spiritualism, but *possession*." " I was weak and sickly. As I grew up and gained health and strength, all these phenomena ceased."

At the age of 17 she was married to General Blavatsky, for many years Governor of Erivan in Armenia. He was 60 years of age, and she had no affection for him, but married him in a fit of girlish ill humour. She " bolted speedily, after a succession of stormy scenes, from his household, never to return."

Subsequently Madame Blavatsky spent many years in travelling. She led Mr. Sinnett, one of her dupes, to believe that she had displayed her courage by fighting in man's dress, at the battle of Mentana in Italy. Another fiction is that she was several years in Tibet, studying under men of supernatural knowledge, called Mahátmas, or "Great Souls."

In 1872 she was in Cairo in Egypt. She was known there as the Russian Spiritist, who called the dead and made them answer questions. A lady, who afterwards married a person named Coulomb, had recently lost a brother. She went to Madame Blavatsky and tried to get some information about him; but she neither saw nor heard anything except a few raps. When she mentioned her disappointment to the Secretary of the Society, he said that the spirits did not like to appear in a room which had not been purified; but if she came back in a few days, she would see wonders. A room was being prepared to be used solely for consulting spirits. When Madame Coulomb returned one day, she found the place filled with people abusing Madame Blavatsky for cheating them of their money, and showing them only a long glove stuffed with cotton, said to represent the hand and arm of some spirit. The Foundress of Theosophy afterwards expressed a wish that the page which described her Cairo experience might be "torn out of the book of her life."

Madame Blavatsky in America.

From Egypt Madame Blavatsky returned to Russia. After spending some time there, she went to America, where she became a naturalized American.

On October 14, 1874, Colonel Olcott first met Madame Blavatsky at Chittenden, in the house of the Eddy Brothers, two farmers. The brothers were supposed to be able to communicate with spirits, and people wrote to them asking what lottery tickets they should buy, whether a certain enterprise would be successful, when some one would get married, and other questions like those put to astrologers in this country. By means probably of a magic lantern, they professed to show ghosts or spirits from another world.

Madame Blavatsky wished to start a Society. For this purpose she needed the help of a gentleman in good position to act as its President. For this purpose she selected Colonel Olcott. His other qualification was the "voracious credulity" with which he charges a large body of spiritualists. (page 4).

Madame Blavatsky, in collusion with the Eddy Brothers, played tricks upon Colonel Olcott. He thus describes the first of the Russian lady's spirit visitors:—

"He was a person of middle height, well-shaped, dressed in a Georgian (Caucasian) jacket, with loose sleeves and long pointed over sleeves, an outer long coat, baggy trousers, leggings of yellow leather and white skull-cap or fez, with tassel. She recognised him at once as Michalko Guiegidze, late of Kutais." *

But on the evening of October 24th, there was a much more remarkable manifestation. When the light was extinguished, the ghost of George Dix, a sailor who had been drowned, thus spoke to Madame Blavatsky:

"Madame, I am now about to give you a test of the genuineness of the manifestations in this circle, which, I think, will satisfy not only you, but a sceptical world beside. I shall place in your hands the buckle of a medal of honour worn in life by your brave father, and buried with his body in Russia. This has been brought to you by your uncle, whom you have seen materialised this evening."

Colonel Olcott says:

"Presently I heard the lady utter an exclamation, and, a light being struck, we all saw Mme. de B. holding in her hand a silver buckle of a most curious shape which she regarded with speechless wonder.

"Was there ever a 'manifestation' more wonderful than this? A token dug by unknown means from a father's grave, and laid in his daughter's hand, 5,000 miles away, across an ocean! a jewel from the breast of a warrior sleeping in his last sleep in Russian ground, sparkling in the candle light in a gloomy apartment of a Vermont farm-house!"†

The explanation is that the buckle was never in the grave.

---

* *People from the Other World*, p. 355.   †|*Ibid*, p.

It had been given by Madame Blavatsky to the Eddy Brothers to deceive Colonel Olcott.

Colonel Olcott saw another wonderful " manifestation :"

"Hands of various sizes were shown. Among them one was too peculiar to be passed over. It was a left hand, and upon the lower bone of the thumb a bony excrescence was growing, which Madame de Blavatsky recognised and said was caused by a gun shot wound in one of Garibaldi's battles."*

Colonel Olcott candidly admits that when he saw the "spirits, or what purported to be such, in every imaginable variety of costume, the light has been dim—very dim—and I have not been able to recognise the lineaments of a single face. I could not even swear to the lineaments of certain of my personal friends who presented themselves." "One cannot, with untrained eye, distinguish accurately between forms varying as much as six inches in height."† Madame Blavatsky must have been gifted with acute sight to recognise the "bony excrescence on the lower bone of the thumb."

Madame Blavatsky led Colonel Olcott to believe that she held intercourse with Mahatmas or " Brothers," Masters in magical art. One of them had been induced to accept Colonel Olcott as a pupil, and letters received through Madame Blavatsky were alleged to have been written by them. One day a woman, strangely dressed and veiled, brought a letter from the "Brothers," and handed it to Madame Blavatsky. It was discovered afterwards that this supposed Spirit Messenger was an Irish servant girl, to whom Madame Blavatsky had promised 5 dollars (about Rs. 10) for personating the Messenger. Having failed to get the money, she confessed the fraud.

On another occasion, a person was dressed up as a Mahatma, and came to the room where the Colonel was sitting. As a proof of his visit, he left his turban, which the Colonel retains to this day.

Madame Blavatsky acquired such an influence over Colonel Olcott, that she wrote of him as a "psychologised baby," "who did not know his head from his heels."

ESTABLISHMENT OF THE THEOSOPHICAL SOCIETY.

Colonel Olcott, the "President-Founder" of the Society, says: "On the 17th November, 1875, I had the honor of delivering in the City of New York, my inaugural address as President of the Theosophical Society."

The objects of the Society was said to be as follows:

First.—To form the nucleus of a Universal Brotherhood of Humanity, without distinction of race, creed, or color.

---

* *People from the Other World*, p. 315. † *Ibid*, pp. 163, 164.

Second.—To promote the study of Aryan and other eastern literatures, religions, and sciences, and vindicate their importance.

Third.—To investigate the hidden mysteries of nature and the psychical powers in man.

*The third was the grand object until the imposture was discovered.

Theosophists have been sailing under false colours. The name *theosophy* is a misnomer. The word is derived from *theos*, God, and *sophos*, wise. The proper meaning is divine wisdom. It was originally used to express a more intimate knowledge of the relation of the soul with God. As will hereafter be shown, the Founders were avowed atheists. Their Theosophy is therefore ATHEOSOPHY, godless wisdom. But the *Chicago Religio-Philosophical Journal* suggests a still better name, BLAVATSKOSOPHY, Blavatsky wisdom!

Theosophy is now explained to mean the WISDOM RELIGION. Its effects are just the reverse.

The course of the Society in America was by no means smooth. In his first Indian lecture, Colonel Olcott admits that during the Society's four years of activity in America, there were "foes all about, public sentiment hostile, the press scornful and relentless;" "the press has lampooned us in writing and pictorial caricature." (p. 1). Colonel Olcott was ridiculed as the "Hierophant;" Madame Blavatsky was called "the champion impostor of the age."* The *New York Sun* thus "chaffed" the "President-Founder":—

"While the 'Hierophant' was still a resident of the Eighth Avenue, he had full faith in the capacity of an industrious Theosophist to attain through contemplation, initiation, and a strictly virtuous life the power of defying and overcoming what are generally accepted as the laws of nature. He believed in levitation, for example, but when we invited him to illustrate his faith by stepping out of an upper window of the *Tribune* tall tower, he was fain to admit that this was a height of adept science which he had not yet attained, and to master which a journey to the Himalayas was necessary."

The Americans were too sharp for Theosophy to succeed. Colonel Olcott, at the anniversary address in Bombay, in November, 1879, says, "of the thirteen officers and councillors elected at the meeting (17th November 1875), only three remain; the rest having dropped off for one reason or another and left us to carry on our work with new associates who replaced them." (p. 18).

When a person plunges head foremost into the water and comes up again at a little distance, he is said to "take a header." Colonel Olcott and Madame Blavatsky, as one of their associates expresses it, wisely "took a header," and turned up in Bombay on the 16th February, 1879.

---

* *The Occult World*, p. 152.

THE THEOSOPHICAL SOCIETY IN INDIA.

Preparedness of India for Theosophy.

"Ghosts," it has been said "are almost the first guess of the savage, almost the last infirmity of the civilised imagination."* But India is one of the countries where "occult phenomena" are likely to find most ready credence. The Hindus claim to have 64 arts and sciences. The following are some of them :—

13. The science of prognosticating by omens and augury.
14. Science of healing, which may include restoration to life of the dead, the reunion of severed limbs, &c.
15. Physiognomy, chiromancy, &c.
36. The art of summoning by enchantment.
37. Exorcism.
38. Exciting hatred between persons by magical spells.
41. The art of bringing one over to another's side by enchantment.
42. Alchemy and chemistry.
44. The language of brute creatures from ants upwards.
47. Charms against poison.
48. Information respecting any lost thing obtained by astronomical calculations.
50. The art of becoming invisible.
51. The art of walking in the air.
52. The power of leaving one's own body and entering another lifeless body or substance at pleasure.
56. Restraining the action of fire.
57. The art of walking upon water.
58. The art of restraining the power of wind.
62. The art of preventing the discovery of things concealed.
63. The art by which the power of the sword or any other weapon is nullified.
64. The power of stationing the soul at pleasure, in any of the five stages.*

The so-called "pandits" of India accept the above "sciences" as true: what, then, may be expected of the masses? Lyall says, "It is probable that in no other time or country has witchcraft ever been so comfortably practised as it is now in India under British rule."†

The intellect of the people has been so dwarfed by Hinduism, that they believe the grossest absurdities. The wild fictions of the Ramayana are generally accepted as true. To obtain medicine, the monkey god Hanuman brought through the air a great mountain from the Himalayas; the sun was hidden by him in one of his armpits.

The field chosen was therefore peculiarly favourable to the growth of Theosophy.

---

* *Encyclopædia Britannica*, Vol. II.   † *Asiatic Studies*, p. 96.

History of the Society, 1879—1884.

Bombay.—The first Theosophist party landed at Bombay on the 16th February, 1879. It consisted of Colonel Olcott, Madame Blavatsky, Miss Bates and Mr. Wimbridge. The two latter were English by birth, who had become members only a few weeks before the party left America for India. Some time during the year, they were joined by M. and Madame Coulomb, old Egyptian acquaintances of Madame Blavatsky.

Colonel Olcott's first address, giving an account of the "Theosophical Society and its Aims," was delivered at the Framji Cowasji Hall on March 23. The first year seems to have been spent in Western India. "The Fourth Anniversary Address was delivered in November 1879." The Society's Monthly Periodical, *The Theosophist*, was started the previous month.

In concluding his second address, Colonel Olcott said :—

"There is one regret that comes to mar the pleasure of this evening, and somewhat dim the lustre of all these lamps—our Buddhist brothers of Ceylon are absent. And absent too, is that most beloved Teacher of ours, that elder brother, so good, so erudite, so good, so courageous—Swamiji Dayânand Sarasvati." (p. 28.)

First Visit to Ceylon.—The Theosophists paid their first visit to Ceylon in May, 1880. Colonel Olcott thus describes his welcome, and contrasts it with Indian experience :—

"During our visit of 1880, the Sinhalese people *en masse* gave us a princely reception. We moved through the Island from Galle to Kandy and back again, in almost a 'royal progress.' They exhausted their ingenuity to do us honour, as in the ancient days they had done to their kings. Triumphal arches, flags flying in every town, village and hamlet, roads lined with *olla* fringes for miles together; monster audiences gathered together to hear and see us. These evidences of exuberant joy and warm affection astounded us."

There is no doubt that a white *gentleman*, and still more a white *lady*, avowing themselves Buddhists, created a great sensation among the Sinhalese.

North India.—Colonel Olcott and Madame Blavatsky, after their return from Ceylon, went, about August 1880, to North India. The former delivered a lecture on "Spiritualism and Theosophy," at Simla, on October 7th, and one on "India, Past, Present and Future" at Amritsar, on the 29th of the same month. They did not return to Bombay till the last day of the year.

During this visit the famous "brooch incident" happened, which will afterwards be described. Their reception seems to have been almost as enthusiastic as in Ceylon. Colonel Olcott, in a letter published in America, and dated Umballa, Punjab, Nov. 26th, writes:

"I am going to spend a week with the Maharajah of Benares and will then return to Bombay. . . . . Things are booming along splendidly. It is a rare thing for us to be able to travel around as we do for nothing. It is a good thing that it is so, as I have not got a cent. Neither has Blavatsky."

Bombay in 1881.—On the 27th February, 1881, Colonel Olcott gave a lecture in Bombay on "Theosophy : its Friends and Enemies." On the 18th April, Madame Blavatsky, Acting Treasurer, presented a statement of the Society's receipts from Dec. 1, 1878 to April 30, 1881. Initiation fees had been received from 108 persons in India, from 246 in Ceylon, and 30 in Europe, realising Rs. 3,900 ; various other sources yielded Rs. 2,973-3-4. The total expenditure, including passages from New York to Bombay, amounted to Rs. 26,419-6-5. The difference between the receipts and expenditure, amounting to Rs. 19,546-3-1, was "advanced as a loan without interest or security," by Colonel Olcott and Madame Blavatsky.*

Second Visit to Ceylon.—Colonel Olcott proceeded to Ceylon in April, where he remained till mid-December, including a visit to Tinnevelly in October. He thus describes the results :—

"During these 212 days I gave sixty public-addresses at temples, school houses, colleges and in the open air; held two conventions, or councils of Buddhist priests, travelled hundreds of miles, within the Western Province ; largely increased the membership of our Society; wrote, published, and distributed 12,000 copies of Buddhist Catechism ; had translated into the Sinhalese language several freethought tracts; and raised by national subscription the sum of about Rs. 17,000 as the nucleus of a National Buddhistic Fund, for the promotion of the Buddhist religion, and the establishment of schools.' (pp. 121-2).

Colonel Olcott and four Sinhalese members came over to Tinnevelly in October, where they met with a grand welcome. The Sinhalese planted a cocoa-nut in a Hindu temple as a mark of respect. The temple was subsequently purified, as usual after visits by Europeans.

Sixth Anniversary.—Colonel Olcott's Sixth Anniversary Address was delivered at Bombay, on January 12th, 1882.

He spoke thus plainly :—

"We have got beyond the preliminary stage of polite phrases on both sides. You know just how we keep our promises, and we know what yours are worth. The scented garlands Bombay brought us in February 1879, withered long ago, its complimentary speeches of welcome long since died away the air." (p. 116).

The initiation fees from 1st May to 31st December 1881, amounted to Rs. 1,838, and a donation of Rs. 100 was received. The expenditure amounted to Rs. 6,529.

The following month Colonel Olcott gave a lecture in the Bombay Town Hall, on "The Spirit of the Zoroastrian Religion."

Visit to Calcutta.—The late Babu Peary Chand Mittra, of Calcutta, had been a spiritualist for many years. Partly through

---

* Supplement to *The Theosophist*, May 1881.

his influence, Colonel Olcott, when he visited that city in March, 1882, met with a warm reception. At a *soiree* given by the Hon. Maharajah Jotendro Mohun Tagore, C. S. I., Babu Peary Chand Mittra thus addressed Colonel Olcott :—

"I welcome you most heartily and cordially as a brother. Although you are of American extraction, yet, in thought and feeling, in sympathy, aspirations, and spiritual conception, you are a *Hindu*; and we, therefore, look upon you as a brother in the true sense of the word.... It is for the promotion of the truly religious end that you, brother, and that most exalted lady, Madame Blavatsky, at whose feet I feel inclined to kneel down with grateful tears, have been working in the most saint-like manner, and your reward is from the God of all perfection."*

A Society was established, with Babu Peary Chand Mittra as President.

First Visit to Madras.—Colonel Olcott and Madame Blavatsky landed at Madras from Calcutta on the 23rd April, 1882. An address of "*Welcome*," signed by several hundred influential native gentlemen was read, and the Hon. Humayun Jah Bahadoor, C. S. I., placed wreaths of flowers around their necks. A large villa at Mylapore, a suburb of Madras, was placed at their disposal. After visiting different parts of the Presidency, Colonel Olcott and Madame Blavatsky left in June for Bombay. In his farewell address Colonel Olcott thus spoke of their reception :—

"We have learnt by experience what a Madras welcome means, and how much generous cordiality is included in the Madrassee's notion of hospitality to the stranger. I make no invidious comparisons when I say, that we, whom you have entertained like blood relations rather than like guests, will remember your attentions and your politeness as among the highest features of not only our Indian, but even of our whole experiences." (p. 205).

Third Visit to Ceylon.—Colonel Olcott landed in Ceylon for the third time, in July 1882. During his visit he delivered 64 lectures, and collected for the Sinhalese National Buddhistic Fund Rs. 6,807, for whose management a Board of Trustees was appointed. During his visit he is said to have "healed more than fifty paralytics, in each case using the name of Lord Buddha."† He returned to Bombay about the end of October.

Seventh Anniversary.—This was celebrated at Bombay on the 7th December, 1882. "An unusual dignity was given to the occasion by the presence in the chair of Mr. A. P. Sinnett, author of 'The Occult World.' Around the Hall were suspended 39 metal shields, painted blue, upon which were inscribed the names of the branches of our Society, which have been founded in Asia. Behind the President-Founder, a sepoy held the beautiful banner which has just been worked for the Society by Madame Coulomb."‡

---

* Supplement to *The Theosophist*, May, 1882.
† *The Theosophist*, April, 1883, p. 159.
‡ Supplement to *The Theosophist*, January, 1883.

The Treasurer's Report from 1st January to 4th December, 1882, was submitted. The Admission Fees realised Rs. 4,163; Donations, Rs. 190. The chief items of Expenditure were Head-quarter's Maintenance, Rs. 4,571, Travelling Expenses, Rs. 3,417. The total Expenditure amounted to Rs. 8,906. The cash advanced by Madame Blavatsky and Colonel Olcott, was Rs. 4,553.

Removal of Headquarters to Madras.—From Colonel Olcott's reference to the "withered garlands" of Bombay, it would appear that the progress of the Society in Western India had not been very satisfactory. The Southern Presidency seemed to present a more hopeful field, and towards the close of 1882 a change was made. A house was selected in the Southern suburb, called Adyar, and it was hoped that sufficient funds would be raised to enable it to be purchased for the Society. How far this expectation was eventually realised, the writer does not know. In October the following appeared:

"The Founders headed the list with a cash donation of Rs. 500, highly approving of the project—although they expect to have to advance about Rs. 5,000 this year besides. Well, out of Rs. 8,520 (all necessary repairs excluded) hitherto only Rs. 3,200 are paid. The sacred fire of devotion and enthusiasm that burned so brightly at the beginning has flickered away, and the probable consequences are that we will have to pay the rest ourselves."*

Bengal Tour.—This seems to have lasted from 23rd February to 19th May, 1883. It is remarkable for its "astounding cures." Col. Olcott's Acting Private Secretary reports 2,812 cases treated. Some details of them are given. Other incidents during 1883 were the "Open Letter" of Colonel Olcott, to the Bishop of Madras, the "peremptory orders" from the 'Paramaguru' stopping Colonel Olcott's healing; the doubling of a lady's ring at Ootacamund, and the restoration by the "Brothers" of a broken China tray at Madras.

EXPOSURE OF THE PHENOMENA IN 1884.

Leading Events during 1884.—The Theosophist party had been joined by Dr. Hartmann, from California, and Mr. W. Q. Judge, of New York. Colonel Olcott, after appointing a Special Executive Committee to transact business during his absence, left Bombay for Marseilles, with Madame Blavatsky, on the 20th February, for the benefit of their health and to further the objects of the Society. Meetings were held in London and in different parts of the Continent of Europe.

While Madame Blavatsky was in Europe, the Theosophists at the Madras head-quarters quarrelled among themselves, and turned out two of their number, M. Coulomb and his wife. There is a proverb, "When rogues quarrel their knaveries come to light," and

---
* Supplement to *The Theosophist*, October, 1883.

so it happened in this case. Madame Coulomb had for several years been a great friend of Madame Blavatsky, and had a large number of letters written to her, some of them explaining how she was to assist Madame Blavatsky in her tricks.

Madame Coulomb gave all these letters to the Rev. George Patterson, Editor of the *Madras Christian College Magazine*. As they proved unmistakably that Madame Blavatsky was a trickster, plagiarist,* forger, and liar, trying to deceive ignorant people in India, the Editor, after careful examination, published an account of the fraud. Dr. Miller and the other Professors of the Madras Christian College agreed with him. Madame Blavatsky asserted that the letters were, in whole or in part, forgeries; but when challenged to prove this in a court of law, she prudently declined.

There is a Society in England, called the "Psychical Research Society." *Psychical* comes from the Greek word *psychē*, the soul. It is intended to investigate questions connected with the mind, including mesmerism, &c. The President is Professor Sidgwick of Cambridge, author of the well known treatise, *The Method of Ethics*.

The Society had heard of the wonders attributed to Madame Blavatsky and of their exposure by the *Christian College Magazine*. To ascertain the truth, Mr. R. Hodgson, a Cambridge graduate, was sent out to India, where he spent three months in investigating the evidence for the so-called "phenomena" or wonders.

Mr. Hodgson carefully examined Madame Blavatsky's letters, which were also subsequently submitted to experts in London who considered them undoubtedly genuine. He questioned a number of witnesses. Among them was Mr. A. O. Hume, "Father of the National Congress," in whose house Madame Blavatsky had lived some months. Mr. Hume had found out Madame Blavatsky's trickery, and had given up all dealings with her.

Mr. Hodgson took Madame Blavatsky's letters to Europe, and wrote out a long account of his investigations. All were submitted to the Committee of the Society, and, after careful consideration, Professor Sidgwick wrote the Report in which the "phenomena" were said to be fraudulent, and Madame Blavatsky was characterised as a clever "impostor" or cheat.

Madame Blavatsky claimed to have lived several years in Tibet as the Chela, or disciple of a Mahatma, and to have partly acquired some of his magical powers. Careful inquiry showed that her pretended "phenomena" were mere tricks. An explanation of the manner in which they were performed will now be given.

---

* One who claims other people's writings as his own.

EXPLANATION OF MADAME BLAVATSKY'S FRAUDS.

DISCOVERY OF A BROOCH.

A brooch is an ornamental pin, worn by ladies, generally to fasten some article of dress. At a dinner party at Simla in the house of Mr. A. O. Hume, Madame Blavatsky asked Mrs. Hume whether there was anything she particularly wished for. She mentioned an old family brooch which had been lost. In the course of the evening Madame Blavatsky said that she had, by her occult power, seen the brooch fall into a bed of flowers in the garden. On search being made, the brooch was found, the fact being attested by nine witnesses.

The explanation of this is the following:

Mrs. Hume gave the brooch to her daughter, who gave it to a young gentleman whom she expected to marry. This gentleman resided for some time in Bombay in the same house with Madame Blavatsky. Needing money, he sold the brooch; Madame Blavatsky obtained it, took it with her to Simla, and hid it in the flower-bed where it was found.

The natives of India have long been familiar with feats akin to the "Brooch Incident." When an ingenious Brahman wishes to earn an easy livelihood, one expedient is to bury beforehand an image in the ground. He does not profess to be "clairvoyant," like Madame Blavatsky, but uses the more commonplace device of a dream. The god appears to him in a vision of the night, informs him that an image, miraculously produced, is to be found buried in such and such a field, and that a temple should be built upon the spot. In the morning, he makes known the revelation he has received, and the principal men of the village are asked to go to the place. On digging, the image is found, of which a declaration might be made before any notary public. The temple is built, and the Brahman is installed as its officiating priest, entitled to the offerings made at the shrine.

CUP AND SAUCER.

One morning Madame Blavatsky accompanied a few friends on a picnic among the hills. There were originally to have been only six persons, but a seventh joined the party before starting. When they came to the place for breakfast, there were only six cups and saucers for seven people. One of the party suggested that Madame Blavatsky should create another cup. She said that it would be very difficult, but she would try. After wandering about a little, and pretending to speak to her Mahatma, she pointed out a place where they would be found. On digging, first a cup and then a saucer was found. The cup and saucer both corresponded exactly in pattern with those brought for the picnic.

The explanation is the same as the foregoing.

Madame Blavatsky was living in the house with the party giving the picnic. It was easy for her to obtain a cup and saucer of the same pattern. These were previously buried, and found when she pointed out the place.

DOUBLING OF A RING.

"Doubling," or producing another thing of the same kind, is one of the "phenomena" which those skilled in occult science claim to perform. There is a well-known story of a Calcutta Mahatma who professed to double bank notes.

One day a lady at Ootacamund and Madame Blavatsky, warm friends, were sitting together on a sofa. "A sapphire ring was taken from the finger of the lady and almost immediately—two minutes after—restored to her with another, the duplicate of the former, only a great deal larger, and set with a sapphire of greater value than the original."

It should be observed that the cup and saucer corresponded exactly, while the ring did not, being larger and set with a stone of greater value than the original. Why should there be this difference? The explanation is that the former belonged to the same set, while Madame Blavatsky had got the ring made in Ceylon, so that, although like, it was not a complete match.

REPAIRING A BROKEN CHINA TRAY.

In the Occult Room* in the Madras head-quarters, there was what was called a Shrine. The Shrine was about 3 or 4 feet in width and height, and about a foot or 15 inches in depth, with a drawer below. The back was formed of three sliding pieces. This was placed against the wall of Madame Blavatsky's bedroom. By means of a hole in the wall, concealed by the shrine, Madame Blavatsky was able to put letters or anything else into the shrine. The opening in her bedroom was concealed by an almirah which could easily be shifted.

Madame Blavatsky wished wealthy people to join the Society that they might give money for its support. She sought to induce them to do so by the exhibition of some of her wonders. Among those whom she thus tried to influence was General Morgan.

General Morgan was invited to see a portrait of the Mahatma Koot Hoomi, contained in the shrine. When the doors were opened, a China tray, leaning against them, fell on the hard chunam floor and was broken. The pieces were carefully collected, tied in a cloth,

---

* *Occult* means hidden, secret.

placed within the shrine, and the doors locked. General Morgan remarked that the Mahatmas if they chose, could easily restore the broken article. After five minutes, the doors were unlocked, and on opening the cloth, the China tray was found whole and perfect without a trace of the breakage!

Madame Blavatsky was at Ootacamund, but she had made the arrangements beforehand with Madame Coulomb, and had sent a note professedly from the Mahatma Koot Hoomi, in which it was said that " the mischief is easily repaired. K. H."

Madame Coulomb was ordered to buy two China trays of the same pattern. The shopkeeper's bill was produced and examined by Mr. Hodgson. One tray was placed from behind leaning against the door, so that it fell when opened. It could not have been so placed in front. When the broken pieces were placed inside the cloth, they were removed through the hole in the wall, and the whole China tray was substituted.

Bell Sounds in the Air.

Colonel Olcott refers to " sweet music coming from afar." A leading Madras Theosophist adduces " bell sounds in the air" as evidence of the truth of the system.

The sound is produced by a contrivance which Madame Blavatsky concealed under her clothing. When pressed by her arm against her side, the sound was produced, louder or fainter according to the pleasure. It may be brought at any good shop in London where conjuring apparatus is sold.

Sending Cigarettes.

Madame Blavatsky was a great smoker. The cigarette papers she which always carried about with her, were supposed to be " impregnated with her personal magnetism." " The theory is that a current of what can only be called magnetism can be made to convey objects previously dissipated by the same force, to any distance, and in spite of the intervention of any amount of matter."*

One form of this " phenomenon" was to tear a cigarette in two, and mark each end with pencil lines. One end would be given to a person to hold, and shortly after the other would be found inside a piano or in some other part of the room. Mr. Sinnett himself makes the following admission :—

"Of course any one familiar with conjuring will be aware that an imitation of this 'trick' can be arranged by a person gifted with a little sleight of hand. You take two pieces of papers, and tear off a corner of both together, so that the jags of both are the same. You make a cigarette with one piece, and put it in the place where you mean to have it ultimately found.

---

* *Occult World*, p. 62.

You then hold the other piece underneath the one you tear in presence of the spectator, slip in one of the already torn corners into his hand instead of that he sees you tear, make your cigarette with the other part of the original piece, dispose of that anyhow you please and allow the prepared cigarette to be found."*

But sometimes cigarettes were sent to great distances. Madame Coulomb explains how this was arranged. She placed them as directed by Madame Blavatsky, and lo! they were found in every case except one. The *fiasco* occurred at Bombay, where the former had been told to place a cigarette on the statue of the Prince of Wales, but failed. The explanation given was that the rain had washed away the cigarette.†

The above is confirmed by extracts from Madame Blavatsky's letters. She wrote thus to Madame Coulomb:

"I enclose an envelope with a cigarette paper in it. I will drop another *half* of a cigarette behind the Queen's head where I dropped my hair the same day or Saturday. Is the hair still there? and a cigarette still under the *cover?*"

Madame Blavatsky wrote on the fly-leaf of the letter from which this passage is taken:

"Make a half cigarette of this. *Take care of the edges.*"

And on a slip of paper said by Madame Coulomb to have accompanied the cigarette paper referred to:

"Roll a cigarette of this half and tie it with H. P. B.'s hair. Put it on the top of the cup-board made by Wimbridge to the farthest corner near the wall on the right. Do it quick."‡

THE SASSOON TELEGRAM.

Mr. Jacob Sassoon is a very wealthy citizen of Bombay. On this account Madame Blavatsky was very desirous that he should become a Theosophist. He was willing to do so if he could obtain some proof of the existence of Mahatmas. Madame Blavatsky thought that a telegram received from a Mahatma would afford sufficient evidence. She therefore, when at Poona, arranged with Madame Coulomb in Madras as follows:

"Now dear, let us change the programme. Whether *something* succeeds or not I must try. Jacob Sassoon, the happy proprietor of a crore of rupees, with whose family I dined last night, is anxious to become a Theosophist. He is ready to give 10,000 rupees to buy and repair the headquarters; he said to Colonel (Ezekiel, his cousin, arranged all this) if only he saw a little phenomenon, got the assurance that the *Mahatmas* could hear what was said, or give him some *other sign of their existence* (? ! !) Well, this letter will reach you the 26th, Friday; will you go up to the Shrine and ask K. H. (or Christo-

---

* *Occult World*, p. 63.
† *Some Account*, &c. p. 16.
‡ *Proceedings of the Psychical Research Society*, p. 213.

folo) to send me a telegram that would reach me about 4 or 5 in the afternoon, same day, worded thus :—
"Your conversation with Mr. Jacob Sassoon reached Master just now. Were the latter even to satisfy him, still the doubter would hardly find the moral courage to connect himself with the Society."
"RAMALINGA DEB."
"If this reaches me on the 26th, even in the evening, it will still produce a tremendous impression. Address, Care of N. Khandallavalla, Judge, POONA. JE FERAI LE RESTE. Cela coûtera quatre ou cinq roupies. *Cela ne fait rien.*"*

"The envelope which Madame Coulomb shows as belonging to this letter bears the postmarks, Poona, October 24th ; Madras, October 26th ; 2nd delivery, Adyar, October 26th; (as to which Madame Blavatsky has written in the margin of my Copy of Madame Coulomb's pamphlet) some Account of my Intercourse with Madame Blavatsky): ' cannot the cover have contained another letter ? (Funny evidence !') Madame Coulomb also shows in connection with this letter an official receipt for a telegram sent in the name of Ramalinga Deb from the St. Thomé Office, at Madras, to Madame Blavatsky, at Poona, on October 26th, which contained the same number of words as above." †

The above letter shows Madame Blavatsky's contempt for her dupes. "Give him *some other sign of their existence (? ! !*")

MAHATMAS.

Theosophy professes, not to have originated in Madame Blavatsky's brain, as its enemies insinuate, but in the revelations of Mahatmas, "great souls," who found in her a fit channel for the propagation of ' Truth.'

It has been well said that the alleged existence of Mahatmas, or "Tibetan Brothers," is the most "inexplicable phenomenon" connected with Theosophy. An ex-Theosophist remarked : " If the Brothers are a myth, the Society for me is moonshine."

The proofs of their existence are threefold :

I. THEIR ALLEGED APPEARANCE.

A sight of one of the "Brothers" was ardently desired by some influential members of the Society. It was considered the one thing necessary to shut the mouths of gainsayers. Madame Blavatsky therefore tried to meet their wishes. Madame Coulomb gives the following account of the manner in which this was effected :—

"She cut a paper-pattern of the face I was to make, which I still have;

---
* The words in French are: I WILL DO THE REST. It will cost 4 or 5 rupees *That is nothing.*"
† *Proceedings of the Psychical Research Society*, p. 211.

on this I cut the precious lineaments of the beloved Master, but to my shame I must say that after all my trouble of cutting, sewing and stuffing, Madame said that it looked like an old Jew—I suppose she meant Shylock. Madame with a graceful touch here and there of her painting brush gave it a little better appearance, but this was only a head without bust and could not very well be used, so I made a jacket which I doubled and between the two cloths I placed stuffing to form the shoulders and chest. The arms were only up to the elbow, because when the thing was tried on we found the long arm would be in the way of him who had to carry it."*

M. Coulomb, one moonlight night, appeared on the balcony of the house, wearing this mask, and leaning against the balustrade. At the same time he dropped a letter. Colonel Olcott and Damodar signed a certificate, testifying to the appearance of the "Illustrious" in his astral body. At an "entertainment," given in the Old College Hall, Madras, Madame Coulomb produced the mask, which corresponded fairly well with Colonel Olcott's account.

Colonel Olcott acknowledges that American mediums make use of "puppets." The thing is conceivable that they might be employed by Madame Blavatsky. The manifestations of the "Brothers" were usually so fleeting, that those who saw them might very easily have been mistaken. They were not seen under "test conditions."

The Theosophists, like the Spiritualists mentioned by Colonel Olcott, (page 4,) consider that the mask was prepared "by the unbelievers themselves to strike a blow at their holy cause."

II. Their Letters.

The Mahatmas have chiefly distinguished themselves by their replies to letters addressed to them. It is a reproduction of the old system of oracles, which may therefore be briefly noticed.

Oracles.—These date from the remotest antiquity, but gradually declined with the increase of knowledge. Many of the Egyptian temples were oracular. The following is a brief account of Greek oracles:—

"Ancient literature shows the Greeks as a people whose religion ran much into the consultation of oracle gods at many temples, of which the shrine of Apollo at Delphos was the chief. No rite could keep up more perfectly the habit of savage religion than their necromancy, or consulting ghosts for prophecy; there was a famous oracle of the dead near the river Acheron in Thesprotia, where the departing souls crossed on their way to Hades."†

When the writer visited the temple of "Isis" "unveiled" at Pompeii, a secret entrance to the shrine was pointed out, by means of which responsive oracles were given to the "imbeciles" of those days.

---

* Some Account, p. 81.   † Encyclopædia Britannica, Vol. XV.

The chief of the Mahatmas, Koot Hoomi, seems to have been first brought on the stage by means of Mr. Sinnett. Through a "happy inspiration," he was led to address a letter "to the Unknown Brother." From "that small beginning," says Mr. S., "has arisen the most interesting correspondence in which I have ever been privileged to engage."

The first Brother to whom Madame Blavatsky applied did not wish to be troubled; another was more obliging. Mr. Sinnett gives the following account of his new correspondent:—

"He was a native of the Panjab who was attached to occult studies from his earliest boyhood. He was sent to Europe whilst still a youth at the intervention of a relative—himself an occultist—to be educated in Western knowledge, and since then has been fully initiated in the greater knowledge of the East.

"My correspondent is known to me as Koot Hoomi Lal Sing. This is his 'Thibetan mystic name'—occultists, it would seem, taking new names on initiation."

The name is said to be "Thibetan." An expert at the British Museum Library examined a recent Thibetan Dictionary, and found no such words as "Koot" and "Hoomi." The most eminent Panjabi scholar of the day writes, "Koot Hoomi is a name, I believe, to be quite unknown in the Panjab. I have been here about fifty years and I have never heard anything like it."

Mr. Lillie says:—

"*The Occult World* (p. 65) tells us Koot Hoomi is a native of the Panjab, and, *Isis Unveiled* tells us he is a native of Kashmir (Vol. II., p. 609). We learn also that he is a Kutchi and the 'son of a Katchi.' *Ibid*, Vol. II., p. 628."*

These accounts with regard to his nationality are rather conflicting. He has now been wisely placed in Tibet, where he cannot be cross-examined.

Mr. Sinnett admits that there is "a foolish suspicion entertained by some sceptics" that the letters supposed to come from the Brothers were written by Madame Blavatsky. Mr. C. C. Massey, who in 1880 was one of the Society's Vice-Presidents, writing in 1882, mentions that it had been "maliciously suggested" that Koot Hoomi is an alias for Madame Blavatsky. He has since withdrawn from the Society, it is believed because he considers the "malicious" suggestion to be correct.

The following are some of the reasons for attributing the authorship of the letters to Madame Blavatsky, and not to an imaginary "Brother."

1. **Handwriting and Paper.**—Madame Blavatsky acknowledges that when young, she could write in a peculiar old-fashioned German hand.† Her acquaintance with Russian, French, &c., would also easily enable her to have different styles of penmanship.

---

* *Koot Hoomi Unveiled*, p. 14.   † *Esoteric Philosophy*, No. 1, p. 87.

The writer has seen only one specimen of writing alleged to be by one of the "Brothers." It is in blue pencil. It is rather curious that Mr. Sinnett refers to Madame Blavatsky "fingering a blue pencil."* He also notices another coincidence. "The pink paper on which it was written (a letter from a Brother) appeared to be the same which Madame Blavatsky had taken blank from her pocket shortly before."†

2. **Style.**—Koot Hoomi was educated in England, but, like Webster's Dictionary, he spells "scepticism" with a *k*. Madame Blavatsky assured Mr. Sinnett that this "was not an Americanism in his case, but due to a philological whim of his"!‡

The language of good American writers, like Washington Irving, is as pure and chaste as that of English authors. In the United States, however, where political struggles are very keen, there is a style of mock eloquence, called "stump oratory." Referring to this, *The Saturday Review* characterises Koot Hoomi's letters as "Choice American." *The Bombay Gazette* expresses a similar opinion:

"As yet the sage has unfortunately only revealed himself to his worshippers in a series of letters whose vulgar and inflated style makes us shudder at the prospect before us, if Occultism is destined to become the world's religion. The new revelation, so far, is like nothing so much as a series of leading articles from a third-rate American paper." *Sept.* 24, 1881.

3. **Subject Matter.**—Like the ancient oracles and the spiritualistic replies received by Dr. Hartmann, the letters of the Mahatmas or Brothers are generally very vague. A clever fortune-teller can often worm out secrets from her dupes, so as to lead them to suppose that she possesses preternatural knowledge. Madame Blavatsky knew well the persons who sought to communicate with the Brothers, and could easily prepare letters suited to their cases.

From the "priceless treasures of their researches,"§ the Brothers have not communicated a single jewel worthy of preservation. Old time-worn platitudes are simply presented in a "Brummagem" setting.

4. **Koot Hoomi's Plagiarisms.**—Mr. Kiddle, an American professor, on reading "The Occult World," says:

"I was greatly surprised to find in one of the letters presented to Mr. Sinnett as having been transmitted to him by Koot Hoomi in the mysterious manner described, a passage taken almost *verbatim* from an address on Spiritualism by me at Lake Pleasant in August, 1880, and published the same month by the *Banner of Light*. As Mr. Sinnett's book did not appear till a considerable time afterwards (about a year, I think), it is certain that I did not quote, consciously or consciously from its pages. How, then, did it get into Koot Hoomi's mysterious letter?"

---

* *Occult World*, p. 95. ‡ *Ibid*, p. 78.
† *Ibid*, p. 44. § *Ibid*, p. 5.

The following are the passages referred to, printed side by side for the sake of ready reference :—

Extract from Mr. Kiddle's discourse entitled "The Present Outlook of Spiritualism," delivered at Lake Pleasant camp meeting, on Sunday, August 15th, 1880.	Extract from Koot Hoomi's letter to Mr. Sinnet, in "The Occult World," 3rd edition, p. 102. The first edition was published in June, 1881.
"My friends, *ideas* rule the world, and as men's minds receive new ideas, laying aside the old and effete, the world advances. Society rests upon them; mighty revolutions spring from them; institutions crumble before their onward march. It is just as impossible to resist their influx, when the tide comes, as to stay the progress of the tide."	"Ideas rule the world; and as men's minds receive new ideas, laying aside the old and effete, the world will advance. Mighty revolutions will spring from them, creeds and even powers will crumble before their onward march, crushed by their irresistible force. It will be just as impossible to resist their influence when the time comes as to stay the progress of the tide."

If the papers of two students at a University examination contained passages corresponding so closely as the above, it would certainly concluded that one copied from the other or that both copied from the same original.

5. **Koot Hoomi's Excuses.**—A liar often tries to support one falsehood by another. One of the best means of convicting him is to examine his supposed evidence.

Koot Hoomi's first excuse is,

"I was physically very tired by a ride of forty-eight hours consecutively, and (physically again) half asleep."*

If Koot Hoomi could come in his "astral body" from Thibet to Bombay, how was the poor man obliged to be "48 hours consecutively" in the saddle ?

The second reason alleged is as follows :—

"It was dictated mentally in the direction of and precipitated by a young chela not yet expert in this branch of psychic chemistry, and who had to transcribe it from the hardly visible imprint. Half of it, therefore, was omitted, and the other half more or less distorted by the 'artist.'"

If the "young chela" had written something different from Mr. Kiddle's remarks, it could easily be understood, but that he should copy sentences almost *verbatim* is certainly an "occult phenomenon."

Koot Hoomi afterwards admitted that the extracts given were quotations; but even this is unsatisfactory. The Report of the Psychical Research Society says :—

"More lately (in *Light*, September 20th 1884), Mr. Kiddle has shown that the passage thus restored by no means comprises the whole of the unac-

---

* *Occult World*, p. 145.

knowledged quotations; and, moreover, that these newly-indicated quotations are antecedent to those already admitted by Koot Hoomi, and described as forming the introduction to a fresh topic of criticism. The proof of a deliberate plagiarism aggravated by a fictitious defence is therefore irresistible."

* Koot Hoomi himself affords the true explanation. "I was not then anticipating its publication." He thought that his plagiarism would never be detected.

6. **Channel of Communication.**—This was through Madame Blavatsky. Two leading Theosophists, who thought that the Society might be better managed, wished to write straight to the "Brothers." One of the latter says :—

"Your desire is to be brought to communicate with one of us directly, without the agency of Madame Blavatsky or any medium."*

As might be expected, this audacious proposal was condemned by Koot Hoomi, in a long letter, as "*selfish!*"† All letters through the astral post must go through the recognised postmistress. Any other course would have been "unreasonable."

7. **Place of Reception.**—Such phenomena *usually* took place at the headquarters. Dr. Hartmann says :—

"Many of the 'occult letters' that were received,—but by no means all—were received either in that cupboard or in Madame Blavatsky's rooms. The cupboard was a sort of post-office, to mail and receive letters from the Masters."‡

For the first two or three months after Madame Blavatsky left for Europe, a few letters were received about the same time as the overland mails, but afterwards they seem to have entirely ceased. Enemies of the cause derided the oracle as dumb; Koot Hoomi was accused of deserting his friends when his help was most required. A more charitable conjecture was that he had himself been "precipitated" down some Himalayan *khud*. Such accidents are not unusual on the mountains, and might easily happen to a man half asleep and exhausted with a 48 hours' ride.

8. **Manner of Reception.**—This is an important element.

Letters were usually dropped, but at Madras a "shrine" was specially made for them by Deschamps.

Mr. Judge, in his lecture delivered at the request of some Madras students, says :—

"They held meetings in closed rooms, and yet objects would come through the ceiling. Tyndall, Huxley and others might say that such a thing was impossible, but the lecturer said he had seen such things happen. ... The lecturer had seen letters drop."

When Mr. Sinnett was at the Society's head-quarters, Bombay, a letter dropped suddenly on the table in the middle of the room. Why had a shrine to be made at Madras? Mr. Judge notwith-

---

* *Occult World*, p. 70.   † *Ibid*, pp. 71-74.   ‡ *Report of Observations*, p. 13.

standing, it would appear that Tyndall and Huxley were right in thinking that letters could not come through a thick Madras ceiling, composed of brick and mortar. In Bombay, houses have usually boarded floors and cloth ceiling. Letters could easily be made to drop through a Bombay floor, while such a course was impossible at Madras. Madame Coulomb gives an account of a trap which was fixed on the floor of the garret above Mr. Sinnett's room; the floor was a boarded one, and between the boards was a space sufficiently wide to permit a thick letter to slip through easily. By pulling a string attached to the trap, the letter could be disengaged at any moment.*

The Madras shrine stood in the "Occult Room," which was next to Madame Blavatsky's bed-room.

Dr. Hartmann bears witness to the following :—

"Besides this hole in the wall there were found to be three secret openings or sliding panels in various places. One into the occult room, opening into the back of another cupboard or book-case, whose front was covered by a mirror and which was made accessible from the hall."†

The explanation given by the Theosophists is that " all these tricks, holes, and trap-doors" were the work of M. Coulomb and his wife after Madame Blavatsky left in order to criminate her. M. Coulomb asserts that they were made by her orders, and her enemies say that she used them to put letters in the shrine. As *The Christian College Magazine* puts it : "*primâ facie*, it is more likely that letters and saucers should be pushed through sliding panels and secret passages than through stout teak wood planks and solid masonry walls."‡

When "Koot Hoomi" is "Unveiled," the form disclosed is that of Madame Blavatsky.

3. ALLEGED ASSISTANCE OF THE MAHATMAS IN WRITING "ISIS UNVEILED."

"ISIS UNVEILED" is a work in two thick octavo volumes. It professes to be "A MASTER-KEY TO THE MYSTERIES OF ANCIENT AND MODERN SCIENCE AND THEOLOGY."

Madame Blavatsky gives the following account of its preparation.

"It is but too true that 'the material sadly needs reducing to order,' but it never was *my* province to do so, as I gave out one detached chapter after the other and was quite ignorant as Mr. Sinnett correctly states in the *Occult World*, whether I had started upon a series of articles, one book or two books... Most of the doctrines given had to be translated from an Asiatic language... Most if not all the quotations from and references to, other works,— some of them out of print, and many inaccessible but to the few—and which

---

* Some Account, p. 33. † Report, p. 43. ‡ Oct. 1884.

the author personally had never read or seen, though the passages quoted were proved in each instance minutely correct."*

Mr. Sinnett gives further details:—

"In the production of this book she was so largely helped by the Brothers, that great portions of it are not really her work at all. In the morning she would sometimes get up and find as much as thirty slips added to the manuscript she had left on her table over-night.

"The book was written—as regards its physical production—at New York, where Madame Blavatsky was utterly unprovided with books of reference. It teems, however, with references to books of all sorts, including many of a very unusual character, and with quotations the exactitude of which may easily be verified at the great European libraries, as foot-notes supply the number of the pages, from which the passages taken or quoted."†

If the above account is correct, Mr. Sinnett rightly terms the book a "great phenomenon." It may justly complete with Bacon's treatise to be called *maximus partus temporis*, the greatest birth of time!

Mr. Arthur Lillie, in "Koot Hoomi Unveiled," gives a very different account. According to him, it is largely translated from *Dogme et Ritual de la Haute Magie*, written, by Louis Constant, a French ex-priest, under the name of Eliphas Lévi. The geological part of it is said to be derived from Donelly's *Atlantis*. A clue is thus afforded to what astonished Mr. Sinnett. Any one may make a show of learning by copying references to works which he "had never read or seen," and they may be "proved in each instance minutely correct." What is novel in this case, is that the prodigy is attributed to the aid of Mahatmas.

The Saturday Review, one of the first literary journals in England, characterises *Isis Unveiled* as a "mystical jumble." In a review of the work which appeared in the *St. James's Gazette*, July 30th, 1884, Madame Blavatsky's ignorance is represented as astounding. "Almost every page shows this ignorance."

The gross ignorance of Madame Blavatsky and the Mahatmas who assisted her is shown by Mr. W. E. Coleman in a series of papers which appeared in the *Chicago Religio-Philosophical Journal* in 1889. The following is an extract from the issue of August 31st:—

"The Bhagavad Gita is the gem of Sanskrit literature ..... One would think that if there was any Sanskrit book with which Madame Blavatsky would be familiar, not in the original, for she was and is no Sanskritist, but in translation, it would be the Gita. But when she wrote *Isis* she did not even know the name of the book, and was in ignorance of its contents. In a large number of places in *Isis* she speaks of this book which she calls the *Bagaved gita*. Note the difference in spelling between this and *Bhagavad Gita*. None but a Sanskrit ignoramus would omit the 'h' after the initial 'B,' or spell Gita, with two 't's.' There are no such words in Sanskrit as Bagaved and Gitta, (See *Isis Unveiled*, ii. 199, 257, 275, 277, 405.) So much for the name; now for the contents of the book. *I. U.* ii. 199, states that the

---

* *The Theosophist*, Vol. II, p. 258.   † *The Occult World*, pp. 80, 109.

whole story of the massacre of the children at the birth of Jesus in Matthew was 'bodily taken' from the Bagaved gitta. There is not a word in the Bhagavad Gita about the slaughter of children at the birth of Krishna, to which she refers. *I. U.* ii. 257, states that the Bagaved gitta contains an account of Vishnu assuming the form of a fish to reclaim the Vedas lost during the deluge, and in ii. 405 is found a purported quotation from the Bagaved gitta concerning the deluge. Nothing of this, in any form or manner, is in the Gita. The truth is that Madame Blavatsky has confounded two very different books, the Bhagavad Gita and the Bhagavad Purana. The things which she claims to be in the Gita are in the Purana. In another place she twice speaks of the Bhagavatta (ii. 260), the name of which she spells wrongly, using two 't's' in it instead of one. It is plain that Madame Blavatsky had never seen either of these books, the Gita or Purana. Her information concerning and quotations from them were copied from Lewis Jacolliot's writings. He was her standard authority. As is well known, Jacolliot's works are full of forgeries and blunders, utterly worthless productions; and yet he is Madame Blavatsky's principal authority on Hinduism and Sanskrit literature in *Isis*. That work is full of forgeries from Sanskrit works, adopted and copied as truth from Jacolliot.

"A woman who does not know the difference between the Bhagavad Gita and the Bhagavata Purana, and who cannot spell the name of either correctly, and who adopts Jacolliot as her principal authority, is indeed a reliable writer on Hinduism and Sanskrit literature!!"

Numerous other illustrations are given of her ignorance of Hinduism. The following is a similar example so far as Buddhism is concerned :—

"We read in *I. U.* i. 92 that Maha Maya, or Maha Deva, the mother of Gautama Bhudda (*sic*) had the birth of her son announced to her by Bhôdisât (*sic*)......The name Maha Deva is so common in Hindu literature, as an appellation of Shiva, the third member of the Hindu triad or trimurtti, that it would seem that the veriest smatterer in Hinduism should know better than to call Buddha's mother Maha-Deva. Moreover, no woman could be called Maha-deva in Sanskrit. Deva in Sanskrit is masculine; the feminine is Devi; and Gautama's mother Maya is sometimes called Maha-Devi; but never Deva."

The above opinion is supported by the high authority of Professor Max Müller, Editor of the *Rig-Veda* and of the *Sacred Books of the East* :—

"There is nothing that cannot be traced back to generally accessible Brahmanic or Buddhistic sources, only everything is muddled or misunderstood. If I were asked what Madame Blavatsky's Esoteric Buddhism really is, I should say it was Buddhism misunderstood, distorted, caricatured. There is nothing in it beyond what was known already, chiefly from books that are now antiquated. The most ordinary terms are misspelt and misinterpreted." *The Nineteenth Century*, May, 1893, p. 775.

REPORT OF THE PSYCHICAL RESEARCH SOCIETY.

This Society was founded in 1882, under the Presidency of Professor H. Sidgwick of Cambridge, author of *The Method of Ethics*, &c. Its object is to make "an organised attempt to investigate that large group of debatable phenomena designated by such terms as mesmeric, psychical, and spiritualistic." Some distinguished men are connected with it. The following Report was written by Professor Sidgwick. It is followed in the Proceedings* by " 2. Account of Personal Investigations in India, and discussion of the Authorship of the " Koot Hoomi" Letters, by Richard Hodgson."

Mr. Hodgson's " Account" occupies 193 pages, and contains " Plan of Occult Room with Shrine and Surroundings," together with *fac, similes* of a number of the Letters.

STATEMENT AND CONCLUSIONS OF THE COMMITTEE.

In May, 1884, the Council of the Society for Psychical Research appointed a Committee for the purpose of taking such evidence as to the alleged phenomena connected with the Theosophical Society as might be offered by members of that body at the time in England, or as could be collected elsewhere.

The Committee consisted of the following members, with power to add to their number:—Messrs. E. Gurney, F. W. H. Myers, F. Podmore, H. Sidgwick, and J. H. Slack. They have since added Mr. R. Hodgson and Mrs. H. Sidgwick to their number.

For the convenience of Members who may not have followed the progress of the Theosophical Society, a few words of preliminary explanation may be added here.

The Theosophical Society was founded in New York in 1875, by Colonel Olcott and Madame Blavatsky, ostensibly for certain philanthropic and literary purposes. Its headquarters were removed to India in 1878, and it made considerable progress among the Hindus and other educated natives. "The Occult World," by Mr. Sinnett, at that time editor of the *Pioneer*, introduced the Society to English readers, and that work, which dealt mainly with phenomena, was succeeded by " Esoteric Buddhism," in which some tenets of the Occult Doctrine, are so-called " Wisdom-religion," were set forth. But with these doctrines the Committee have, of course, no concern.

The Committee had the opportunity of examining Colonel Olcott and Madame Blavatsky, who spent some months in England in the summer of 1884, and Mr. Mohini M. Chatterji, a Brahman graduate of the University of Calcutta, who accompanied them. Mr. Sinnett also gave evidence before the Committee ; and they have had before them oral and written testimony from numerous other members of the Theosophical Society in England, India, and other countries, besides the accounts of phenomena published in

---

* December, 1885. Published by Trübner & Co. Price 4s. 6d.

"The Occult World," "Hints on Esoteric Theosophy," *The Theosophist*, and elsewhere.

According to this evidence, there exists in Tibet a brotherhood whose members have acquired a power over nature which enables them to perform wonders beyond the reach of ordinary men. Madame Blavatsky asserts herself to be a *Chela* or disciple of these Brothers, (spoken of also as *Adepts* and as *Mahatmas*,) and they are alleged to have interested themselves in a special way in the Theosophical Society, and to have performed many marvels in connection with it. They are said to be able to cause apparitions of themselves in places where their bodies are not, and not only to appear, but to communicate intelligently with those whom they then visit, and themselves to perceive what is going on when their phantasm appears. This phantasmal appearance has been called by Theosophists the projection of the "Astral form." The evidence before the Committee includes several cases of such alleged appearances of two Mahatmas, Koot Hoomi and Morya. It is further alleged that their chelas, or disciples, are gradually taught this art, and that Mr. Damodar K. Mavalankar in particular, a Theosophist residing at the head-quarters of the Society, has acquired it, and has practised it on several occasions. It may be observed that these alleged voluntary apparitions, though carrying us considerably beyond any evidence that has been collected from other sources, still have much analogy with some cases that have come under the notice of the Literary Committee.

But we cannot separate the evidence offered by the Theosophists for projections of the "Astral form," from the evidence which they also offer for a different class of phenomena, similar to some which are said by Spiritualists to occur through the agency of mediums, and which involve the action of "psychical" energies on ponderable mattter; since such phenomena are usually described either as (1) accompanying apparitions of the Mahatmas or their disciples, or (2) at any rate as carrying with them a manifest reference to their agency.

The alleged phenomena which come under this head consist—so far as we need at present take them into account— in the transportation, even through solid matter, of ponderable objects, including letters, and of what the Theosophists regard as their duplication; together with what is called "precipitation" of handwriting and drawings on previously blank paper. The evocation of sound without physical means is also said to occur.

In December, 1884, the Committee considered that the time had come to issue a preliminary and provisional Report. This Report, on account of its provisional character, and for other reasons, was circulated among Members and Associates of the Society for the Psychical Research only and not published. In drawing up the present Report, therefore, the Committee have not assumed that their readers will be acquainted with the former one. The conclusion then come to was expressed as follows: "On the whole (though with some serious reserves), it seems undeniable that there is a *primâ facie* case, for some part, at least, of the claim made, which, at the point which the investigations of the Society for Psychical Research have now reached, cannot, with consistency, be ignored. And it seems plain that an actual residence for some months in India of some trusted observer—by actual intercourse with the persons concerned, Hindu and European, so far as may be permitted to him—is an almost necessary pre-requisite of any more definite judgment.

In accordance with this view, a member of the Committee, Mr. R. Hodgson, B. A., Scholar of St. John's College, Cambridge, proceeded to India in November, 1884, and after carrying on his investigations for three months, returned in April, 1885.

In the *Madras Christian College Magazine* for September and October, 1884, portions of certain letters were published which purported to have been written by Madame Blavatsky to a M. and Madame Coulomb, who had occupied positions of trust at the head-quarters of the Theosophical Society for some years, but had been expelled from it in May, 1884, by the General Council of that Society during the absence of Madame Blavatsky and Colonel Olcott in Europe. These letters, if genuine, unquestionably implicated Madame Blavatsky in a conspiracy to produce marvellous phenomena fraudulently; but they were declared by her to be, in whole or in part, forgeries. One important object of Mr. Hodgson's visit to India was to ascertain, if possible, by examining the letters, and by verifying facts implied or stated in them, and the explanations of the Coulombs concerning them, whether the letters were genuine or not. The Editor of the *Christian College Magazine* had already, as Mr. Hodgson found, taken considerable pains to ascertain this; but he had not been able to obtain the judgment of a recognised expert in handwriting. Accordingly, a selection of the letters, amply sufficient to prove the conspiracy, was entrusted by the editor (in whose charge Madame Coulomb had placed them), to Mr. Hodgson, who sent it home before his own return. These, together with some letters undoubtedly written by Madame Blavatsky, were submitted to the well-known expert in handwriting, Mr. Netherclift, and also to Mr. Sims of the British Museum. These gentlemen came independently to the conclusion that the letters were written by Madame Blavatsky. This opinion is entirely in accordance with the impression produced in the Committee by the general aspect of the letters, as well as by their characteristic style, and much of their contents.

The Committee further desired that Mr. Hodgson should, by

cross-examination and otherwise, obtain evidence that might assist them in judging of the value to be attached to the testimony of some of the principal witnesses; that he should examine localities where phenomena had occurred, with a view of ascertaining whether the explanations by trickery, that suggested themselves to the Committee, or any other such explanations, were possible; and in particular, as already said, that he should, as far as possible, verify the statements of the Coulombs with a view to judging whether their explanations of the phenomena were plausible. For it is obvious that no value for the purpose of the psychical research can be attached to phenomena, where persons like the Coulombs have been concerned, if it can be plausibly shown that they might themselves have produced them: while, at the same time, their unsupported assertions that they did produce them, cannot be taken by itself as evidence.

After hearing what Mr. Hodgson had to say on these points, and after carefully weighing all the evidence before them, the Committee unanimously arrived at the following conclusions:—

(1) That of the letters put forward by Madame Coulomb all those, at least, which the Committee have had the opportunity of themselves examining and of submitting to the judgment of experts, are undoubtedly written by Madame Blavatsky; and suffice to prove that she has been engaged in a long-continued combination with other persons to produce by ordinary means a series of apparent marvels for the support of the Theosophic movement.

(2) That, in particular, the Shrine at Adyar, through which letters purporting to come from Mahatmas were received, was elaborately arranged with a view to the secret insertion of letters and other objects through a sliding panel at the back, and regularly used for this purpose by Madame Blavatsky or her agents.

(3) That there is consequently a very strong general presumption that all the marvellous narratives put forward as evidence of the existence and occult power of the Mahatmas are to be explained as due either (*a*) to deliberate deception carried out by or at the instigation of Madame Blavatsky, or (*b*) to spontaneous illusion, or hallucination, or unconscious misrepresentation, or invention on the part of witnesses.

(4) That after examining Mr. Hodgson's report of the results of this personal inquiries, they are of opinion that the testimony to these marvels is in no case sufficient, taking amount and character together, to resist the force of the general presumption above mentioned.

Accordingly, they think that it would be a waste of time to prolong the investigation.

As to the correctness of Mr. Hodgson's explanation of particular marvels, they do not feel called upon to express any definite conclusion; since on the one hand, they are not in a position to endorse every detail of this explanation, and on the other hand, they have satisfied themselves as to the thoroughness of Mr. Hodgson's investigation, and have complete reliance on his impartiality, and they recognise that his means of arriving at a correct conclusion are far beyond any to which they can lay claim.

There is only one special point on which the Committee think themselves bound to state explicitly a modification of their original view. They said in effect in their First Report that if certain phenomena were not genuine, it was very difficult to suppose that Colonel Olcott was not implicated in the fraud. But after considering the evidence that Mr. Hodgson has laid before them as to Colonel Olcott's extraordinary credulity, and inaccuracy in observation and inference, they desire to disclaim any intention of imputing wilful deception to that gentleman.

The Committee have no desire that their conclusion should be accepted without examination, and wish to afford the reader every opportunity of forming a judgment for himself. They therefore append Mr. Hodgson's account of his investigation, which will be found to form by far the largest and most important part of the present Report. In it and the appendices to it, is incorporated enough of the evidence given by members of the Theosophical Society to afford the reader ample opportunity of judging of both its quantity and quality.

There is, however, evidence for certain phenomena which did not occur in India and are not directly dealt with in Mr. Hodgson's Report. Accounts of them will be found at page 382, with some remarks on this by Mrs. H. Sidgwick.

The Report of Mr. Netherclift on the handwriting of the Blavatsky-Coulomb letters will be found at page 381. Extracts from the letters themselves are given in Mr. Hodgson's Report, pages 211-216.

The authorship of the letters attributed to Koot Hoomi, which are very numerous, and many of them very long, is fully discussed in Mr. Hodgson's Report. It may be mentioned here that it is maintained by some that the *contents* of these letters are such as to preclude the possibility of their having been written by Madame Blavatsky. This has never been the opinion of the Committee, either as regards the published letters or those that have been privately shown to them in manuscript. Those who wish to form an independent opinion on the subject are referred to "The

Occult World" and "Esoteric Buddhism," which contain many of the letters themselves, and much matter derived from others.

In this connection may be conveniently mentioned what the Committee, in their First Report, called the most serious blot which had then been pointed out in the Theosophic evidence. A certain letter, in the Koot Hoomi handwriting and addressed avowedly by Koot Hoomi from Thibet to Mr. Sinnett, in 1880, was proved by Mr. H. Kiddle, of New York, to contain a long passage apparently plagiarised from a speech of Mr. Kiddle's made at Lake Pleasant, August 15th, 1880, and reported in the *Banner of Light* some two months or more previous to the date of Koot Hoomi's letter. Koot Hoomi replied (some months later) that the passages were no doubt *quotations* from Mr. Kiddle's speech, which he had become cognisant of in some occult manner, and which he had stored in his mind; but that the appearance of plagiarism was due to the imperfect precipitation of the letter by the chela, or disciple, charged with the task. Koot Hoomi then gave what he asserted to be the true version of the letter as dictated and recovered by his own scrutiny apparently from the blurred precipitation. In this fuller version the quoted passages were given as quotations, and mixed with controversial matter. Koot Hoomi explained the peculiar form which the error of precipitation had assumed by saying that the quoted passages had been more distinctly impressed on his own mind by an effort of memory than his own interposed remarks; and, that inasmuch as the whole composition had been feebly and inadequately projected, owing to his own physical fatigue at the time, the high lights only, so to speak, had come out; there had been many illegible passages which the Chela had omitted. The Chela, he said, wished to submit the letter to Koot Hoomi for revision, but Koot Hoomi declined for want of time.

The weakness of this explanation was pointed out (in *Light*) by Mr. Massey, who shewed (among other points) that the quoted sentences seemed to have been ingeniously twisted into a polemical sense, precisely opposite to that in which they were written.

And more lately (in *Light*, September 20th 1884), Mr. Kiddle has shown that the passage thus restored by no means comprises the whole of the unacknowledged quotations; and, moreover, that these newly-indicated quotations are antecedent to those already admitted by Koot Hoomi, and described as forming the introduction to a fresh topic of criticism. The proof of a deliberate plagiarism aggravated by a fictitious defence is therefore irresistible.

In conclusion, it is necessary to state that this not the only evidence of fraud in connection with the Theosophical Society and Madame Blavatsky, which the Committee had before them, prior to, or independently of, the publication of the Blavatsky-Coulomb correspondence. Mr. C. C. Massey had brought before them evidence which convinced both him and them that Madame Blavatsky had, in 1879, arranged with a medium, then in London, to cause a "Mahatma" letter to reach him in an apparently "mysterious" way. The particulars will be found at page 397.

It forms no part of our duty to follow Madame Blavatsky into other fields. But with reference to the somewhat varied lines of activity which Mr. Hodgson's Report suggests for her, we may say that we cannot consider any of them as beyond the range of her powers. The homage which her immediate friends have paid to her ability has been for the most part of an unconscious kind; and some of them may still be unwilling to credit her with mental resources which they have hitherto been so far from suspecting. For our own part, we regard her neither as the mouthpiece of hidden seers, nor as a mere vulgar adventuress; we think she has achieved a title to permanent remembrance as one of the most accomplished, ingenious, and interesting impostors in history.

EFFECTS OF THE REPORT.

"Consequent upon the publication of the Hodgson Report," says Mr. W. Emmette Coleman, "the production of phenomena was tabooed in the Theosophical Society; and since then the occultic marvels of the mahatmas, Mme. Blavatsky, and Damodar have ceased. Save an occasional letter from one or other of the adepts, said to have been received by the theosophic leaders, no sign of their existence, or of the possession by them or H. P. B., of occult power has been given. The psychical fraudulence till then rampant in Theosophy was effectually killed by Mr. Hodgson."

Madame Blavatsky was publicly challenged to prove the letters to be forgeries, but she prudently declined, and left India for good. In 1887 she settled in London and started a Theosophical Magazine, called *Lucifer, the Light-bringer*. The following year she published in two volumes, *The Secret Doctrine; the Synthesis of Science, Religion and Philosophy*. This was the means of introducing to her Mrs. Annie Besant, her most important disciple, of whom an account will now be given. The sketch is chiefly compiled from her own writings, and from an account of her life written by her intimate friend, Mr. Stead, which appeared in the *Review of Reviews* in October, 1891.

MRS. ANNIE BESANT.
CHILDHOOD.

Mrs. Annie Besant's maiden name is Wood. She was born in 1847, and is now therefore about 47 years of age. Her father belonged to an English family; but he was born and educated in Ireland, where he took his degree as a doctor, although he seldom practised. Afterwards he removed to London, where he held a good appoinment. Dr. Wood married an Irish lady called Morris. He died in 1852 when his daughter was only five years old. Grief made Mrs. Wood's raven hair white as snow in a single night. Though left a widow with a young family and scarcely any means, instead of seeking help from relations, she nobly sought to earn her own living, and to carry out the dying wish of her husband to give their eldest boy a University education.

Mrs. Wood removed from London to Harrow, where there is one of the most celebrated public schools in England, largely attended by the children of wealthy families. The Rev. Dr. Vaughan, then Headmaster of Harrow, allowed her to take some of the Harrow boys into her own house, so that she was not only able to support herself, but to find means for the education of her son. Mrs. Besant acknowledges that Dr. Vaughan and his wife were the earnest friends and helpers of her mother.

Annie, brought up as a child among boys, was as good a cricketer and climber of trees as any of them. The house had a large garden. There was not a tree in it which she did not climb. One wide-spreading tree was her sitting room and study. She would sit there reading for hours. Milton's *Paradise Lost* was her favourite book. She says, "I liked to personify Satan and declaim the grand speeches of the hero-rebel."

Miss Marryat, a rich benevolent lady, offered to educate Annie free of charge. Mrs. Besant thus acknowledges her obligations to her: "No words can tell how much I owe her, not only of knowledge, but of that love of knowledge which has remained with me ever since as a constant spur to study."

Miss Marryat "visited the poor, taking help wherever she went, and sending food from her own table to the sick." She was an earnest Christian. Annie learnt passages from the Bible and hymns for repetition. She was also made to teach in the Sunday School, for Miss Marryat said, "it was useless to learn, if we did not try to teach those who had no one to teach them."

RELIGIOUS CHANGES BEFORE MARRIAGE.

As there are different sects among Hindus, so there are divisions among Christians. All Christians, properly so called, agree on many of the most important points. They believe in the same God, the same Saviour, and accept the Bible. The short statement of belief, usually called the Apostles' Creed, is generally acknowledged.

The two principal divisions of Christians are Roman Catholics and Protestants. Besides disagreeing on some important points of doctrine, they differ in their modes of worship. The Roman Catholic Church has splendidly decorated churches, and its priests wear rich vestments. Among Protestants, the tendency in worship is towards simplicity. But in the Church of England there is a section, called the High Church party, having a leaning, more or less, to the Church of Rome.

Miss Marryat belonged to the Protestant party, and the future Mrs. Besant was brought up under her influence. She had been taught to shun balls where dancing is carried on late at night. When Miss Wood left Miss Marryat and returned to Harrow, she entered with pleasure into the amusements of the world. "She was devoted to archery and croquet, and danced to her heart's delight with the junior masters 'who could talk as well as flirt.'" But a good deal of attention was also devoted to English literature.

About this time there was what is called the High Church Revival in the Church of England. A series of publications was issued, called *Tracts for the Times*, in which Roman Catholic doctrines and forms of worship were advocated. Mrs. Wood had removed to London, where her daughter, who had acquired High Church views, spent much time in making ornaments and arranging decorations for a Mission Chapel.

During three years Miss Wood had passed through three changes, having been Protestant, worldly, or fond of amusements, and High Church, in turn.

Marriage with Mr. Besant.

At the Mission Chapel, Miss Wood made the acquaintance of a young clergyman, the Rev. Frank Besant, a Cambridge graduate, who helped in the Mission, and supported himself as undermaster of Stockwell Grammar School, London. He is the brother of Mr. Walter Besant, the novelist. In December, 1867, when about 20 years of age, she became his wife. She married him, not from love, but because she thought that he, by his office, would bring her nearer to God.

Soon afterwards Mr. Besant obtained a mastership at Cheltenham, in the west of England. There in lodgings his young wife began to write stories for the *Family Herald*, for which she received her first earned money. She also wrote the "Lives of the Black Letter Saints," for which she could not find a publisher. The first pamphlet which she printed was a little tract, Roman Catholic in its tone, which insisted upon the virtue of fasting.

BECOMES A THEIST AND SEPARATES FROM HER HUSBAND.

Lord Hatherley, Lord Chancellor of England, was the uncle of Mrs. Besant. Through his favour Mr. Besant was appointed in charge of Sibsey, a parish in Lincolnshire, with an income of about £450 a year.

Meanwhile, doubts about some of the truths of Christianity had arisen in her mind. She read both Christian works on the Evidences and Anti-Christian books without any benefit. As a last resolve, she sought the advice of Dr. Pusey, considered the leader of the High Church Party. He did not understand her case, and the interview did more harm than good.

One of the most sacred Christian ordinances is that called the Holy Communion, in memory of the death of Christ. When it was observed at Sibsey, Mrs. Besant walked out of Church. Kind farmers' wives who were present thought she was unwell, and called next day with sympathising inquiries.

Mrs. Besant acted more conscientiously than educated Hindus, who take part in idolatrous ceremonies which they condemn, merely to please their ignorant relatives.

At Sibsey Mrs. Besant wrote her first controversial tract against Christianity. It was published anonymously, as "by the wife of a beneficed clergyman." Subsequently it was republished as the first chapter of *My Path to Atheism*.

As it was very injurious to Mr. Besant's work as a clergyman for his wife to leave Church in the manner above mentioned, the alternative was put to Mrs. Besant either to remain or to return home. The former seemed a violation of conscience, so she chose the latter.

Mrs. Besant went back to her mother, receiving a small monthly income from her husband. She occasionally earned some money by nursing, and by her pen. She was still a Theist, and attended the lectures of Moncure Conway in London.

ANTI-CHRISTIAN.

After separating from her husband, Mrs. Besant gave much of her time to writing tracts against Christianity. With the exception of a few pages, the whole of *My Path to Atheism* is of the above character. For about twenty years she "waged a pitiless war against her early faith and its adherents." She repeatedly showed this spirit during her first Indian tour.

Atheist and Materialist.

Atheistic thoughts were first awakened in Mrs. Besant's mind in the following manner:

Two children were born, first a boy and then a girl. When the latter was seven months old she had, like other children, an attack of whooping cough. The child suffered severely and seemed at death's door, but recovered. Mrs. Besant says: "There had grown up in my mind a feeling of angry resentment against the God who had been for weeks, as I thought, torturing my helpless baby. More than once the indignant cry broke from my lips, 'How canst Thou torture a poor baby so? Why dost Thou not kill her at once and let her be at peace?'"

Mrs. Besant thought there could not be a God, because her child suffered so much pain. The argument is like that of a man who should say, my watch sometimes goes badly; therefore it cannot have had a maker.

Mrs. Besant should rather have thought, If there is no God, how came my child into existence?

The wisest and best men in all ages have believed in the existence of a great Creator.

One great difference between a bad and a good lawyer is that the former cannot grasp the whole of a case. He dwells upon one small point, while he overlooks the far stronger arguments on the other side. So it is with atheists.

A parent punishes his child for wrong-doing. For this he is to be praised rather than blamed. Most of the suffering in the world is caused by men breaking God's laws, and the pain is intended to teach them to reform.

Granting, however, that there is some misery which we cannot explain, we should set against it the innumerable blessings we receive at God's hand, and be content to wait till we reach His presence and get it explained. We are like a child of two years of age, unable fully to understand the government of a mighty empire.

It was, however, intimacy with the late Mr. Bradlaugh that made Mrs. Besant an avowed atheist.

One day in 1874, Mrs. Besant bought a copy of the *National Reformer*. This led her to go and hear Mr. Bradlaugh's lecture in the Hall of Science. She wrote to him, and was accepted as a member of the National Secular Society, established to spread atheism and materialism. Shortly after she went to meet him, when he said to her, "You have thought yourself into Atheism without knowing it." He saw that she was clever, and a few days later he offered her a small weekly salary, and a place on the staff of the *National Reformer*.

For about 15 years Mrs. Besant laboured with zeal to propagate the above doctrines. When women embrace Atheism, so contrary to their religious nature, they are generally blatant, or noisy in the expression of their views. A gentleman in Ceylon says that he was present in the Hall of Science, London, when, Mrs. Besant stood with a watch in her hand and said : " If there be a God, let Him strike me dead in five minutes."

The Evils of Atheism and Materialism.

Mrs. Besant was so deluded as to believe that Atheism was the path to happiness. The Preface to her book, *My Path to Atheism*, concludes as follows :

"The path from Christianity to Atheism is a long one, and its first steps are very rough and very painful; the feet tread on the ruins of broken faith, and the sharp edges cut into the bleeding flesh; but further on the path grows smoother, and presently at its side begins to peep forth the humble daisy of hope that heralds the spring-tide, and further on the roadside is fragrant with all the flowers of summer, sweet and brilliant and gorgeous and in the distance we see the promise of the autumn, the harvest that shall be reaped for the feeding of man."

The way in which this glorious change is to be brought about is thus explained in her *Constructive Rationalism :*

"Full of hope, full of joy, strong to labour, patient to endure, mighty to conquer, goes forth the new glad creed into the sad grey Christian world; at her touch men's faces soften and grow purer, and women's eyes smile instead of weeping; at last, the heir arises to take to himself his own, and the negation of the usurped sovereignty of the popular and traditional God over the world developes into the affirmation of the rightful monarchy of man." pp. 177, 178.

The golden age is to begin when man, the rightful lord of the universe, takes the throne usurped by God !

She thus wrote of the benefits of Materialism :

"As calmly as the tired child lies down to sleep in its mother's arms, and passes into dreamless unconsciousness, so calmly does the Rationalist lie down in the arms of the mighty mother, and pass into dreamless unconsciousness on her bosom."

Mrs. Besant is a most unsafe religious guide. The results were just the opposite of what she promised.

To deny the existence of God is like to blot out the sun from the heavens. Men are then like young orphan children, left to wander alone, without any father whom they may love or to whom they may look for help in trouble. If there is no hereafter in which the virtuous are rewarded and the wicked punished, men may, without fear, live as they please.

MALTHUSIAN.

Malthus was an English writer who brought out in 1798 an *Essay on the Principles of Population.* He was afterwards Professor of Political Economy and Modern History in the East India Company's College at Haileybury. He held that population tends to increase faster than the means of subsistence, and therefore urged that an increase of population should be checked. The remedy he suggested was late marriages.

In 1877 Mr. Bradlaugh and Mrs. Besant united in publishing a book by an American writer which proposed other means for the above object. While they were fitted to answer this end, experience showed that they might also be used to render seduction and adultery safe from detection, although such was not the intention of the publishers. It also permitted to married people the free indulgence of sensual desires.

The book became the subject of a public prosecution. The jury condemned the book as calculated to deprave public morals. As the defendants refused to give up publishing it, they were sentenced to six months' imprisonment as first class misdemeanants, and fined £200 each. Mr. Bradlaugh appealed on a point of law which was decided in their favour, and the whole proceedings were quashed.

The book was afterwards withdrawn, and replaced by another of a somewhat similar character from the pen of Mrs. Besant.

SPIRITUALIST.

Spiritualism has already been explained. Mrs. Besant's account of her experience is briefly as follows:

"I added Spiritualism to my studies, experimentalising privately, finding the phenomena indubitable, but the explanation of them incredible. The phenomena of clair-voyance, clair-audience, thought-reading, were found to be real."*

Clair-voyance, clear-seeing, is a supposed power of being able to see things not present to the senses. It has been repeatedly disproved by the offer of a bank note, equal in value to Rs. 1,000, to any one who would tell its number when enclosed in an envelope. *Clair-audience*, clear-hearing, is a supposed power of hearing sounds inaudible to others. An instrument, called the *microphone*, has been invented which enables very faint sounds to be heard, as the *microscope* enables very small objects to be seen. A fly can be heard walking like an elephant. *Thought reading* professes to know what other people are thinking about. This is possible to some extent. A child can often read his mother's thoughts; he knows by her face whether she is pleased or angry. Clever men can do more, but the power claimed has not yet been established.

---

* Quoted in *Borderland*, October 1893, p. 174.

THEOSOPHIST.

Madame Blavatsky, in 1888, published a large work in two volumes, called, *The Secret Doctrine*. In 1889 this book was given to Mrs. Besant, by Mrs. Stead, to review. Shortly after, she asked Mr. Stead to give her an introduction to Madame Blavatsky.

When Mrs. Besant called on Madame Blavatsky, she found her seated in a large chair before a table. " My dear Mrs. Besant, I have so long wished to see you," was the salutation. Mrs. Besant sat down, while Madame Blavatsky talked of her travels, all the time rolling cigarettes with her fingers, for she was a great smoker. Before leaving, Madame Blavatsky said, " Oh! my dear Mrs. Besant, if you would only come among us!"

Mrs. Besant thus describes the next meeting:—

"THE CHARGES AGAINST H. P. B.

" And so it came to pass that I went again to Lansdowne road to ask about the Theosophical Society. H. P. Blavatsky looked at me piercingly for a moment: ' Have you read the report about me of the Society for Psychical Research?' ' No I never heard of it so far as I know.' ' Go and read it, and if, after reading it, you come back—well.' And nothing more would she say on the subject, but branched off to her experiences in many lands."

" I borrowed a copy of the report, read and re-read it. Quickly I saw how slender was the foundation on which the imposing structure was built. The continual assumptions on which conclusions were based; the incredible character of the allegations; the most damning fact of all—the foul source from which the evidence was derived. Everything turned on the veracity of the Coulombs, and they were self-stamped as partners in the alleged frauds. Could I put such against the frank fearless nature that I had caught a glimpse of, against the proud fiery truthfulness that shone at me from the clear blue eyes—honest and fearless as those of a noble child? Was the writer of ' The Secret Doctrine,' this miserable impostor, this accomplice of tricksters, this foul and loathsome deceiver, this conjurer with trap-doors and sliding panels? I laughed aloud at the absurdity, and flung the report aside with the righteous scorn of an honest nature that knew its own kin when it met them, and shrank from the foulness and baseness of a lie. The next day saw me at the Theosophical Publishing Company's Office at 7, Duke-Street, Adelphi, where Countess Wachtmeister,—one of the lealest of H. P. B's friends—was at work, and I signed an application to be admitted as Fellow of the Theosophical Society." p. 175.

Mrs. Besant was thus received after joining the Society:—

" On receiving my diploma, I betook myself to Landsdowne-road, where I found H. P. B. alone. I went over to her, bent down and kissed her, but said no word. ' You have joined the Society?' ' Yes.' ' You read the report?'—' Yes.' ' Well?'—I knelt down, before her and clasped her hands in mine, looking straight into her eyes: ' My answer is, will you accept me as your pupil, and give me the honour of proclaiming you my teacher in the face of the world?' Her stern set face softened, the unwonted gleam of tears sprang to her eyes; then, with a dignity more than regal, she placed her hand upon my head: ' You are a noble woman. May Master bless you.'

From that day, May 10, 1889, until now—two years, three and a half months after she left her body—my faith in her has never wavered, my trust in her has never been shaken." p. 175.

An explanation has already been given of the "Charges against Madame Blavatsky" and the "Report" to which reference is made.

It should be observed that before joining the Theosophical Society Mrs. Besant never seems to have sought *God's* guidance. Nor does Madame Blavatsky say, "May *God* bless you," but "May *Master* bless you." Her chief "Master" was Koot Hoomi Lal Singh, an imaginary being, a description of whose "astral body" has already been given.

ANTI-MATERIALIST.

Mrs. Besant was one of the lecturers in the Hall of Science, advocating atheism and materialism. She was not satisfied with the result of her labours. She wrote:—

"I had long been deeply troubled as to the 'beyond' (result) of all my efforts at social and political reform. My own Socialism was that of love, and of levelling up; there was much Socialism that was of hatred; and I often wondered if out of hatred any true improvement could spring. I saw that many of the poor were as selfish and as greedy of enjoyment as many of the rich, and sometimes a cold wind of despair swept over me lest the 'brute in man' should destroy the realisation of the noblest theories."

When speaking for the last time in the Hall of Science she said:

"There are problems in the universe which Materialism not only does not solve but which it declares are insoluble—difficulties in life and mind which Materialism cannot grapple with, and in face of which it is not only dumb, but says that mankind must remain dumb for ever...Was I to refuse to see them because my philosophy had for them no place? do what men have done in every age—insist that nature was no greater than my knowledge, and that because a fact was new it was, therefore, a fraud or an illusion?"

Her inquiry ended in the renunciation of Materialism and adoption of Theosophy. She gave up her connection with Mr. Bradlaugh, and became the disciple of Madame Blavatsky. Mr. Stead truly describes her attitude towards her new Guru:

"She sat at her feet learning like a little child all the lore of the Mahatmas; she was obedient in all things."

Through Storm to Peace.—Mrs. Besant (see page 41) gave a glowing picture of the happiness she felt on accepting materialism. Her satisfaction in rejecting it after embracing Theosophy, was equally great:

"And thus I came through storm to peace, not to the peace of an untroubled sea of outer life, which no strong soul can crave, but to an inner peace that outer troubles may not avail to ruffle—a peace which belongs to the eternal, not to the transitory, to the depths not to the shallows of life. It carried me scathless through the terrible Spring of 1891 when death struck down Charles Bradlaugh in the plenitude of his usefulness, and unlocked the gateway into rest for B. P. Blavatsky. Through anxieties and responsibilities heavy and numerous it has borne me; every strain makes it stronger; every trial makes it serene; every assault leaves it more radiant. Quiet confidence has taken the place of doubt; a strong security the place of anxious dread. In life, through death, to life, I am but the servant of the great Brotherhood, and those on whose heads but for a moment the touch of the Master has rested in blessing can never again look upon the world save through eyes made luminous with the radiance of Eternal Peace."*

Her dependence, it will be seen, is not upon her Creator, but the great Brotherhood, and the Master (Koot Hoomi Lal Singh).

Anti-Malthusian.

It has been mentioned that Mrs. Besant and Mr. Bradlaugh had been associated in the publication of a book which, while it checked population, allowed men the free indulgence of their sensual nature, and could be used to avoid discovery in cases of seduction and adultery.

Mrs. Besant now felt that there was "a more excellent way" for restricting population. She advocated self-control and self-denial as far nobler than self-indulgence. With this object in view she refused to print any more or to sell the copyright of her former work. She says:

"Having taken this step, it is right to take it publicly, and to frankly say that my former teaching was based on a mistaken view of man's nature, treating him as the mere product of evolution instead of as the spirit, intelligence, and will without which evolution could not be." *Review of Reviews*, August 1891, p. 143.

In thus acting up to her convictions, Mrs. Besant deserves warm commendation.

Claimant to be the Second "World's Great Teacher."

Mrs. Besant reverently acknowledged Madame Blavatsky to be the "World's Great Teacher." When the latter died in 1891, the former claimed that the mantle of the prophetess had fallen upon her. The *chela* aspired to her successor. She had been associated with Madame Blavatsky in editing *Lucifer*, of which she now took the whole responsibility. Of all the followers of Madame Blavatsky she was, undoubtedly, by far the best qualified. She had such unbounded belief in her Guru, that she did not consider it necessary to investigate charges against her, although sustained by "irresistible evidence." She accepted with unwavering faith the 'phenomena' exhibited by Madame Blavatsky, and the statements of the

---

* *Autobiography*, concluding paragraph.

Mahatmas about "astral bodies," "the seven Kosmic planes of manifestation," &c, But she claimed *sight* as well as *faith*. When interviewed by the Tanjore correspondent of the *Madras Mail*, she is said to have made the following assertions :—

"Do you believe in what the Theosophists call "phenomena?"
"I do believe in phenomena. They were shown me and their reasons were explained to me by Madame Blavatsky who was my *Guru*, and I understood them as the results of psychic development."
Q. "Have you seen a Mahatma?"
A. "I have."*

Her creed may be summed up in the words : "*I do not believe in a personal God ; the concept is impossible to me,*' but I BELIEVE IN MADAME BLAVATSKY AND THE BROTHERHOOD."

Mrs. Besant, among Theosophists, was unrivalled as an orator. Although she discarded her first guru, Mr. Bradlaugh, for her second, yet, under his guidance she had become an "adept" in managing low class audiences, and had acquired a knowledge of all the arts of clap-trap.

Lastly, she had the Irish love of a fight, and was ready to give the challenge to the whole world, " Will any body trample on the tail of my coat ?"

VISIT TO INDIA.

INDIA, A PREPARED FIELD FOR MRS. BESANT'S CLAIMS.

The Chela wisely followed the example of her Guru in choosing India as her first great field of labour. Sir Monier Williams, the Oxford Professor of Sanskrit, who has devoted a long life to the study of India's sacred literature, thus shows the mental condition to which Hindus have been reduced by that, "highly spiritual religion," their "ancient faith" :—

"Its policy being to check the development of intellect, and keep the inferior castes in perpetual childhood, it encouraged an appetite for exaggeration more monstrous and absurd than would be tolerated in the most extravagant European fairy-tale. The more improbable the statement, the more childish delight it was calculated to awaken. This is more true of the Ramayana than of the Mahabharata; but even in the later epic, full as it is of geographical, chronological, and historical details, few assertions can be trusted. Time is measured by millions of years ; space by millions of miles; and if a battle has to be described, nothing is thought of unless millions of soldiers, elephants, and horses are brought into the field."†

Mrs. Besant might therefore expect to find a large number of "imbeciles," "muffs," "flapdoodle (food for fools) babies." Her expectations were realised. At Bangalore she was hailed as "the

---

* *Madras Mail*, Dec. 2, 1893. † *Indian Epic Poetry*, p. 35.

veritable goddess of Ind, coming from the far off West for the spiritual regeneration of the land." Sir Sheshadri Iyar, the Dewan of Mysore, said she was "the incarnation of Saraswati and their sister."

MRS. BESANT'S OBJECT IN COMING TO INDIA.

This was to persuade credulous Hindus to accept Theosophy as their religion, and Mrs. Besant as its " Great Teacher" in succession to Madame Blavatsky, its Founder.

MRS. BESANT'S FLATTERY TO GAIN HER END.

Flattery is the weak point of the Hindus. The most extravagant compliments are in use among them. " Great King" is a very ordinary term of address; "Lord of the 24 worlds" is not unusual; even blasphemy is sometimes employed.

Colonel Olcott, at the commencement, tried flattery, and laid it on thick enough to please even Hindus. When, however, money promised was not forthcoming, he changed his tune. He spoke of some Hindus as being " blinded by flattery, intoxicated with self-adulation." At his Bombay Anniversary Address in January 1882, he said:

" *You know just how we keep our promises; and we know what yours are worth.*"

Colonel Olcott was a kind of Mr. Facing-both-ways. The *Indian Spectator* said : Theosophy "is all a mist to Pandit Dayanand, wherein the colours of the Vedas, of Buddhism, and Zoroastrianism blend. He cannot say where one begins and another ends, so far as Theosophy is concerned." April 2, 1882.

Madame Blavatsky professed herself a Buddhist in Ceylon; her Chela wisely preferred a larger constituency. Mrs. Besant professes to be an out-and-out Hindu. She believes in the gods of the Hindu pantheon, great and small; she upholds the caste system as a necessary part of the law of *Karma*, those in the lowest caste being there as the result of their former works. " Preserve your idols" is another advice.

Nay, she is reported to have made at Bangalore the following astounding statement:

That she was a Hindu Pandit in a former birth, and is visiting her own land after a sojourn in the West where she was reincarnated to know the nature of the materialistic civilisation of those regions.*

In corroboration of her now being a genuine Hindu, she has adopted the name of *Anna Bhai.*

---

* *The Harvest Field*, January 1894, p. 279.

The following is the dose of flattery administered by Anna Bhai in an address at Tinnevelly :

1. The Hindu theosophy is the best of all philosophies.
2. The Hindus are the wisest of all nations.
3. The Sanskrit language is the best of all languages.
4. Western civilization, with all its discoveries in science, is nothing compared with Hindu civilization.
5. All that is best in the West has been borrowed from India.

This is too strong for a few stomachs, and is rather inclined to act as an emetic; but on the "imbeciles" it has all the soothing delightful feeling of an opiate.

Theosophy alleged to be Ancient Hinduism.

"Hindu Theosophy" is held to be "THE BEST OF ALL PHILOSOPHIES." Hindus may ask in surprise why this was not revealed till the time of Madame Blavatsky. Mrs. Besant answers this question satisfactorily. In a lecture at Trichinopoly, as reported by the correspondent of the *Madras Standard*, (Dec. 8) she said :—

"That the present Vedas are not the whole, but that thousands of Slokas have disappeared. That the latter have not been lost, but they have been taken away by the gods knowing that in the *Kali Yuga* India would be brought under foreign yoke, and fearing that the ignorant foreigner would desecrate the sacred science."

The thousands of the lost slokas had been preserved by Mahatmas in Tibet, who communicated the substance of their precious contents to Mrs. Besant's Guru.

This is a pure fiction, totally opposed to fact. At an early period, before the foot of a foreign invader had touched the soil of India, every verse, every word, every syllable of the Rig-Veda had been carefully counted. The number of verses varies from 10,402 to 10,622 according as a few hymns are included or left out; the number of *padas*, or words, is 153,826; that of the syllables 432,000.*

So far from Theosophy being ancient Hinduism, as already mentioned, it is chiefly derived from a French book of magic by a writer who calls himself Eliphas Levi, from Paracelsus, and other medieval mystics. See *Koot Hoomi Unveiled,* by Arthur Lillie, Member of the Royal Asiatic Society. Mr. W. Emmette Coleman is preparing a work in which this will be substantiated by full quotations.

Theosophy, the Organon to restore India to her Pristine Grandeur.

"In the old days," says Mrs. Besant "India was really great; she was great first in the spiritual life; great first in the grandeur

---

* Max Muller's *Ancient Sanskrit Literature*, p. 221.

of her spiritual knowledge, in the depth of her spiritual knowledge."*

Well may it be said, "How are the mighty fallen!"

What is the cause of India's deep degradation? Contact with Western nations, grovelling in the dust of materialism.

But India is not irretrievably ruined. Krishna says in the Bhagavad Gita: "Whensoever religion fades and irreligion prevails, then I produce myself." His present *avatar*, however, is in female form—the white goddess Saraswati—so says the Dewan of Mysore. Mrs. Besant is to be accepted as the World's "Great Teacher," in succession to Madame Blavatsky.

MRS. BESANT'S THREE GREAT MEASURES FOR THE IMPROVEMENT OF INDIA.

1. THE RESTORATION OF HINDU CIVILIZATION.

Mrs. Besant is reported to have said at Tinnevelly:—

" *Western Civilization, with all its discoveries in science, is nothing compared with Hindu Civilization.*"

Dewan Bahadur R. Ragunath Row says that at Kumbakonum she expressed the following wish :

" *She was anxious to see the Aryan Civilization restored, being the oldest, truest, and best in the world.*"†

Mrs. Besant formed the above estimate of Hindu Civilization after having been only a few days in India. Dr. Bhandarkar is a distinguished Oriental Scholar, who has just retired from the Sanskrit Professorship in the Deccan College at Poona. As a mark of the esteem in which he is held, the Bombay Government lately appointed him Vice-Chancellor of the Bombay University. What is his opinion of the comparative merits of Hindu and Western Civilization? In a lecture in Bombay on the *Critical, Comparative, and Historical Method of Inquiry*, addressing his "Hindu friends," he says :—

" *It is no use ignoring the fact that Europe is far a-head of us in all that constitutes Civilization.*" p. 23.

The case is, Mrs. Besant *versus* Dr. Bhandarkar: Whose opinion is to be accepted?

For a full account of Hindu Civilization, the reader is referred to Mr. R. C. Dutt's *Civilization in Ancient India* in 3 volumes.

A comparison between Hindu and Western Civilization is given in *India Past and Present*, 8vo. 96 pp. Price 2 As. Sold by Mr. A. T. Scott, Book Depôt, Madras.

---

* Address in the Victoria Hall, Madras, December 21, 1893.
† Letter to *The Hindu*, December 28, 1893.

India was never so enlightened as it is at present. The words of Macaulay, with reference to medieval Europe, apply with double force to Ancient India: " We see the multitudes sunk in brutal ignorance, and the studious few engaged in acquiring what did not deserve the name of knowledge."

2. The Substitution of Manu's Laws for the Penal Code, and the Retention of Caste.

Mrs. Besant has made the grand discovery, why India has so often fallen under a foreign yoke.

The correspondent of *The Hindu* gives an account of one of her lectures in the Kumbakonum Town Hall, " full to suffocation." The following is an extract:

"Mrs. Annie Besant said that India was a mighty country so long as the dictates of Manu the Legislator were observed to the letter; but when the spirit of his dictates was forgotten by them, hordes after hordes of foreign conquerors swept over the land and subjugated it." Dec. 7th, 1893.

Instead of that, the effect has been *just the opposite*. Manu's Code is the grand support of Caste, well described by Sir H. S. Maine in *Ancient Law*, as " THE MOST DISASTROUS AND BLIGHTING OF HUMAN INSTITUTIONS." Professor Bhandarkar says:

"*The caste system is at the root of the political slavery of India.*"

The Romans had a maxim, "Divide and conquer." The Brahmans acted upon the same principle. By splitting up the people into numerous sections, they more easily retained their supremacy. "A nation divided against itself," is the proper description of the Hindu race. Hence India has become the easy prey of foreign invaders. Sir Lepel Griffin thinks it would be politic on the part of the British Government to encourage caste.

A new feeling of nationality is springing up among educated Indians, but this is in direct opposition to caste. The " National Congresses," regarded with enthusiasm, would be impossible under Manu's caste regulations. Sudras compose the great majority of the population; but if they had presumed to attend and sit in the presence of the " twice-born," banishment and mutilation would have been the reward of their presumption.

Pandit Sivanath Sastri, after enumerating other evils connected with caste, says:

" 9. *It has made the country fit for foreign slavery by previously enslaving the people by the most abject spiritual tyranny.*"

III. The Preservation of the Ancient Faith.

Mrs. Besant made the following earnest appeal:

"*I plead to you for your old faith. Be not ashamed of the ancient worship. Be not recreant to the ancient faith.*"

In an open air address at Madras she adviced Hindus to keep their idols. People do not destroy the playthings of their childhood. They may not care for them, but their sons or grandsons may.

The most *ancient* worship in India, is probably a black stone, smeared with red-lead to represent blood. Are Hindus not to be ashamed of this?

But the most *general* form of worship is *idolatry*. Of India it may well be said, " The land is full of idols !"

Some educated Hindus, adopting an apology learned from Europeans, allege that idols are only like photographs, serving to remind us of those we love.

To a remark of this kind Mr. Desmukh well replied:

"It is true we like to retain photographs of people we love to remind us of their form and features; but your blocks of stone or your deformed hideous brazen images, bought at a shop in the bazaar, of what sort of Divinity do they remind us?"

Mrs. Besant alleged that the idols are only symbolic. Her Hinduism was then only a few weeks old. Rammohun Roy, born and bred a Hindu, knew better the feelings of the people. What does he say?

"Neither do they regard the images of these gods merely in the light of instruments for elevating the mind to the conception of those supposed beings: they are simply in themselves made objects of worship. For whatever Hindu purchases an idol in the market, or constructs one with his own hands, or has one made under his own superintendence, it is his invariable practice to perform certain ceremonies, called *Pran Pratishtha*, or the endowment of animation, by which he believes that its nature is changed from that of the mere materials of which it is formed, and that it acquires not only life but supernatural powers. Shortly afterwards, if the idol be of the masculine gender, he marries it to a feminine one: with no less pomp and magnificence than he celebrates the nuptials of his own children. The mysterious process is now complete; and the god and goddess are esteemed the arbiters of his destiny, and continually receive his most ardent adoration."

Another excuse is that idols were invented for those who are not possessed of sufficient understanding. If so, it is a most condemnatory proof of the degradation to which Hindus have been reduced by their religion. Rammohum Roy thus replies to this pretext:—

"Permit me in this instance to ask whether every Mussulman in Turkey from the highest to the lowest, every Protestant Christian at least of Europe, and many followers of Cabeer and Nanak do worship God without the assistance of consecrated objects? If so, how can we suppose that the human race is not capable of adoring the Supreme Being without the puerile practice of having recourse to visible objects? I will never hesitate to assert, that His adoration is not only possible and practicable, but even incumbent, upon rational creature."

The ignorant do not need images to remind them of God. They cannot understand His form, for He has none. They can remember their parents when far distant; they can love a benefactor whom they have never seen; they can obey the authority of a Queen-Empress though she never set foot on their soil. They can worship God who is a Spirit in spirit and in truth. Idols are a hindrance, not a help, to true worship. They give most degrading ideas of God.

Instead of listening to the Siren voice of Mrs. Besant, let Hindus obey the earnest call of the late Keshub Chunder Sen :—

"For the sake of your souls and for the sake of the souls of millions of your countrymen, come away from hateful idolatry, and acknowledge the one supreme and true God, our Maker, Preserver and Moral Governor, not in belief only, but in the every-day concerns and avocations of your life. By offering such uncompromising allegiance to Him and dedicating yourselves wholly to His service, you will rescue your own consciences from corruption and sin, and your country from superstition, priestcraft, absurd rites, injurious practices, and horrid customs and usages. By declaring a vigorous crusade against Hinduism, you will lay the axe at the root of the tree of corruption."

Intelligent Indian pantheists usually look upon the deities commonly worshipped as mere fictions of the popular mind. If Mrs. Besant takes this view, then, in the words of Professor Flint, she is guilty of a "conscious alliance with falsehood, the deliberate propagation of lies, a persistent career of hypocrisy."*

HOW MRS. BESANT WAS BEFOOLED.

Messages after the death of Madame Blavatsky.†

The Psychical Research Committee had proved that Madame Blavatsky herself had written the letters professedly come from Mahatmas; but after her death in May, 1891, the same missives continued to be received. This was thought by Mrs. Besant to be a triumphant denial.

Speaking at the Hall of Science in August 30, 1891, she said :—

"You have known me in this hall for 16½ years. You have never known me tell a lie (' No, never,' and loud cheers). I tell you that since Madame Blavatsky left I have had letters in the same handwriting as the letters she received (sensation). Unless you think dead persons can write, surely that is a remarkable fact. You are surprised; I do not ask you to believe me; but I tell you it is so. All the evidence I had of the existence of Madame Blavatsky's teachers of the so-called abnormal powers came through her. It is not so now. Unless even sense can at the same time deceive me, unless a

---

* *Antitheistic Theories*, p. 390.
† Abridged from the *Westminster Gazette*, October 29—November 8, 1894. Many details are omitted. Fac-similes of the messages are also given.

person can at the same time be sane and insane, I have exactly the same certainty for the truth of the statements I have made as I know that you are here. I refuse to be false to the knowledge of my intellect and the perceptions of my reasoning faculties."

Mrs. Besant had satisfied herself of the above propositions by evidential processes as certain as the assurance of her own 'sense' and 'reasoning faculty' that her audience were before her as she spoke. Her evidence will now be examined.

The Disputed Succession.

The American Section of the Society was, to some extent, distinct. Its chief officer was Mr. W. Q. Judge, Vice-President of the Society. He was a lawyer's clerk in Colonel Olcott's brother's office, but came out to India for a time, to assist in the Society's work. He fully conformed to the theosophical plan of flattering the Hindus. Addressing some Madras students, he bore the following testimony to Hindu philosophy of which he knew so little :—

"The great Indian nation produced its Sanskrit. Great consideration was due to this language. It contained Philosophy as refined as Herbert Spencer's, and further it used language that Herbert Spencer could not understand. His very ideas were to be found in Indian philosophy elaborated to such an extent that Spencer would do well to throw his books into the sea and apply himself to the study of Hindu Philosophy." *Madras Mail*, Sept. 29, 1884.

When Madame Blavatsky, died in 1891, the question arose, Who was to succeed her? Mrs. Besant was understood to be designated for the office, but Mr. Judge did not wish his claims to be ignored. When he heard of the death of "H. P. B.," he promptly cabled, "*Do nothing till I come.*" Soon after his arrival, he suggested to Mrs. Besant to consult the Mahatmas. He proposed that they should write a certain question on paper, put it in an envelope, shut that into a certain cabinet in "H. P. B." rooms, and invite the Mahatmas to "precipitate" replies.

Mrs. Besant agreed. Mr. Judge himself wrote the question and closed the envelope, and put it into the cabinet. Mrs. Besant afterwards left the room for a time. After due delay, Mr. Judge took the letter out again. On his showing it to Mrs. Besant, judge of that lady's emotion at the discovery that at the end of the question stood the word "Yes," traced apparently in red chalk, also a little lower down the words

"And Hope"

with the impression, in black carbon of a peculiar seal, representing a cryptograph M. (This appearance is easily produced by holding a seal in candle smoke and impress with that.)

This precipitation was not from Mahatma Koot Hoomi, who usually corresponded with Madame Blavatsky; but from Mahatma Morya, who used to sign himself M., although he did not use a seal. There were only a few scraps of his letters, so that the handwriting could not be tested.

Next morning at a meeting of the 'Inner Group,' at which Mr. Judge took up the position of Senior Chela, to which his services as postman of the Mahatmas well entitled him. He said that he had received a letter in America from Mahatma M., whose contents he could not reveal, but he showed the signature and seal, which exactly resembled that 'precipitated' in the cabinet overnight. He specially begged those persons to take note of the seal, "for" said he, "they might have need to recognise it on some future occasion."

Three days after this (May 27) there was a meeting of the Esoteric Section Council to decide how the section should in future be governed. It was expected that Mrs. Besant should succeed, but Mr. Judge proposed that the Council should dissolve and its powers be delegated to Mrs. Besant *and himself* as joint "Outer Heads." Colonel Olcott was in India, so that his claims could be ignored.

Mrs. Besant was quite content with the position proposed; but other members of the Council might have some objections. When expounding it, she was turning over some papers, out of which fluttered a little slip of paper to which Mr. Judge directed her attention.

The slip of paper bore the words in red pencil—.

"JUDGE'S PLAN IS RIGHT."

Signature and seal as before. Round it went from hand to hand. None questioned that paper and script alike had just been "precipitated" unto their midst by "the Master." Thanks to Mr. Judge's foresight, all were in a position to recognise the seal.

Mr. Judge at once went and took his seat at Mrs. Besant's side, and "Judge's plan" was unanimously adopted!

As the first letters were so successful, others followed. One of the first recipients was Mr. Bertram Keightly, a gentleman whose services to Theosophy had been of a material kind, and whose zeal has more than once been rewarded by gratifying marks of approbation from Tibet. Under date May 29, 1891, the Vice-President wrote to Mr. Keightly:—

"Fear not Bert! Masters watch us, and since May 8 have sent word here in writing."

Close beside the signature of "William Q. Judge" appeared in solemn confirmation the M. signature and seal impression. The message was sent in a very roundabout way, for Mr. Keightly was in Madras, several thousand miles nearer Tibet.

On another occasion Mr. Judge, writing to a brother official, used these words:—

"I believe the Master agrees with me, in which case, I will ask him to put his seal here."

Down at once came the seal!

Story of the Mahatmic Seal.

On the decease of "H. P. B.," Colonel Olcott hurried from India to London, but Mr. Judge had arrived before him. On hearing about the performances of the seal, Colonel Olcott smiled, but said nothing. Its history is as follows:

In 1883, when Colonel Olcott was in the Punjab, passing an Urdu seal-engraver's shop, he asked the man to make a seal, bearing the signature which "H. P. B." identified as that of the "Master of Wisdom," Mahatma Morya. He wished to send it as a present to the Mahatma through "H. P. B."

When the seal was shown to Madame Blavatsky, she objected that it was not quite correct, which was a sufficient excuse for not sending it, and with some other things it was thrown into a despatch box belonging to her. In 1888 it was seen by Mr. Keightly, then staying with her in London. On inquiry what the little brass seal was, the prophetess said,

"Oh, it's only a flap-doodle of Olcott's."

The same year Mr. Judge was also staying with Madame. The seal afterwards disappeared.

The President of the Theosophical Society stared at the impression of his own "flap-doodle" seal on that which purported to be a letter from the Mahatma. He remarked to Judge that he had missed a certain brass seal from among Madame Blavatsky's relics, and described the story of its making. He asked Judge if he had seen the seal? Judge answered in the negative. Upon which the Colonel expressed a hope that "no scoundrel would get possession of it, and use it to give colour to bogus Mahatma messages."

The Mock Inquiry.

The Society in India was not very prosperous, and early in 1892, Colonel Olcott resigned the presidency. Mr. Judge professed sorrow, and got a "message" from the Mahatma countermanding the step taken. Colonel Olcott was overjoyed, and withdrew his resignation.

In July of the same year, however, Mr. Judge at the meeting in London forgot to mention either the Master's message or the Colonel's withdrawal of his resignation, and Mr. Judge, on the motion of Mrs. Besant, was elected President for life.

On the announcement of Judge's election Colonel Olcott wrote to London that there was no vacancy, and he printed in the *Theosophist*, the Master's message which had led him to withdraw his resignation.

Mr. Judge when questioned about the Mahatma's seal, declared that " whether He," (the Master) " has a seal or uses one, is something on which I am ignorant." It was on this statement that he was challenged in the *Theosophist* of April, 1893, in an article signed by Messrs. W. R. Old and S. V. Edge, both T. S. officials (secretaries, Indian section.)

By virtue of their joint position as Outer Heads of the Esoteric section to which they were elected under warrant of the very seal in question, Mrs. Besant and Mr. Judge promptly "suspended" Messrs. Old and Edge from their Esoteric membership.

At the Chicago " Parliament of Religions," Mrs. Besant met Mr. G. U. Chakravarti, the Indian representative of the Theosophical Society. Under his influence, Mrs. Besant was convinced that she had been deluded by Judge, that he had himself written with his own hand the letters to which she had pinned her faith.

The Indian section threatened to secede from the Society if Mr. Judge's presidency were confirmed with the scandal unsifted. Judge himself, when offered the alternative of resigning all his offices quietly or facing a "full publication of the facts," replied in a defiant sense.

Mrs. Besant then offered to adopt the charges, turn prosecutor, and conduct the case against Mr. Judge herself. Colonel Olcott was delighted, and all the evidence and control of the case passed into her hands.

A Judicial Committee of the Society, composed of 11 members, met in London on July 10th 1894, professedly to investigate the charges. The President-Founder, who was in the chair, in a long address gave the following reasons why Mr. Judge could not be tried :

Either the Mahatma letters are genuine or they are fabricated :

(*a*) If found to be genuine, that implies the affirmation of the existence of Mahatmas as a Theosophic dogma, and the abandonment of the Society's precious " neutrality," which is unconstitutional.

(*b*) If found to be bogus missives produced by the Vice-President, then it is obvious that he must have done it in his private capacity ; the production of bogus documents being no part of his official duties. Therefore he cannot be tried by an official tribunal.

Mrs. Besant, like the President, was "convinced that the point was rightly taken." There was nothing more to be said.

On the 12th July, Mrs. Besant made a long statement. She admitted, "I did my utmost to prevent a public Committee of Enquiry of an official character."*

She acknowledged that as stated by the President :—

"The vital charge is that Mr. Judge has issued letters and messages in the script recognizable as that adopted by a Master with whom H. P. B. was closely connected, and that these letters and messages were neither written nor precipitated directly by the Master in whose writing they appear; as leading up to this there are subsidiary charges of deception."

"Further, I wish it to be distinctly understand that I do not charge and have not charged Mr. Judge with forgery in the ordinary sense of the term, but with giving a misleading material form to messages received psychically from the Master in various ways without acquainting the recipients with this fact."

"Forgery in the ordinary sense of the term," means imitating a known person's signature; Mr. Judge was not guilty of this, because the Mahatma M. has no existence.

Mrs. Besant also blamed the "vindictiveness" of Mr. Judges's accusers in pressing an inquiry "painful" to Mr. Judge, and paid laudatory tributes to his character and Theosophical activity.

Down sat Mrs. Besant and up rose Mr. Judge, and read *his* statement. It contained the following sentences :—

"I repeat my denial of the said rumoured charges of forging the said names and handwritings of the Mahatmas, or of misusing the same. I admit that I have received and delivered messages from the Mahatmas...they were obtained through me, but as to how they were obtained or produced I cannot state. ... I willingly say that which I never denied, that I am a human being, full of error, liable to mistake, not infallible, but just the same any other human being."

The following Resolutions, moved by Mr. Keightley, were then adopted :

Resolved : That this meeting accepts with pleasure the adjustment arrived at by Annie Besant and William Q. Judge as a final settlement of matters pending hitherto between them as prosecutor and defendant, with a hope that it may be thus buried and forgotten, and—

Resolved : That we will join hands with them to further the cause of genuine brotherhood in which we all believe."

This mock "Enquiry" in the case of Mr. Judge is a repetition of what took place in Madras after the *Madras Christian College Magazine's* exposure of Madame Blavatsky's frauds. She was exonerated, and recommended not to accept the challenge to prove in a Court of law that the letters were forgeries.

Evidence of Lying and Fraud on the part of Mr. Judge.—Such

---

* Supplement to the *Theosophist* for September 1894, p. xlviii.

serious charges require to be well substantiated. Mr. F. E. Garrett, the author of the articles in *the Westminster Gazette*, says:—

"The evidence for those facts, be it good or bad, is that of the Theosophical leaders themselves, written and signed as the case against the Vice-President, and adopted by Mrs. Besant as true. If it be not true, then Colonel Olcott, Mr. B. Keightley, Mr. W. R. Old, and the other official witnesses must be guilty of a conspiracy, as I said it the outset, 'even more discreditable to the personal of the Society.' It is not I who accuse Mr. Judge. It is Mr. Judge and his colleagues who accuse each other. The rank-and-file of the Theosophists have paid their money; they may now take their choice."

"The fact is, before Mrs. Besant got hold of the evidence, at least one set of complete and duly witnessed copies had been made, together with facsimiles of the documents. It is these which lately fell into my hands, under circumstances which left me free to take, as I do, the moral and legal responsibility of that publication which the President first promised and afterwards shirked."[*]

Opinion of Mr. W. Q. Judge.—"In regard to Mr. William Q. Judge, Vice-president, I do not feel called on to labour any theory of my own as to that gentlemen's character and conduct. As the Society of Psychical Research long ago remarked, the precise line between rogue and dupe in the Theosophical Society has never been easy to draw....With the facts of the preceding narrative before him, the reader can form his own opinion."

Opinion of Mrs. Besant.—"I take Mrs. Besant's statement at the so-called 'Enquiry,' that she believed now that Judge wrote with his own hand the missives which he had induced her, and she had induced the public to regard as precipitations from Tibet of the kind which 'some people would call miraculous.'

"Apparently Mrs. Besant considers that this avowal sufficed to clear her honour towards her colleagues and the public whom she had, 'misled.' To me it appears admirably calculated to mislead them again. Remember even those whom Mrs. Besant was addressing—much more the outside public—were ignorant of the facts. Mrs. Besant had taken good care of that. Had she boldly cut herself free from the rottenness at the core of the Theosophic movement as soon as it was shown to her, she might have saved her reputation for straightforwardness, if not for intelligence. In choosing instead the equivocal policy of hushing up a scandal at all costs, she doubtless convinced herself that she was acting only for the ends of edification and the good of her church. That is the old, old story of priestcraft, and Mrs. Besant has been playing the high priestess now for three years. But were there not also some more personal motives at work? There is one thing which even the most candid hate to confess— and that is, that they have been thoroughly bamboozled. It does not improve matters when they have themselves helped in their own

---

[*] *Westminster Gazette*, Nov. 8, 1894.

bamboozlement. To confess how recklessly inaccurate were her statements about 'the same hand-writing,' the 'semi-miraculous precipitation,' the absolute assurance of her own senses, and so forth; to let the public see for itself the childish twaddle which she accepted and helped to force upon others as profound and oracular: all this would have been a sad come-down from the Delphic tripod. I do not wonder the poor lady shrank from it. I do wonder that Mrs. Besant tried to evade it at the expense of a sort of confidence-trick. To this has come the woman whom we once thought, whatever her other faults, at least fearless and open—the woman whose epitaph, as she tells us, is to be

She Sought to Follow Truth!"*

MRS. BESANT DEPOSED BY "MASTER'S DIRECTION."

While this pamphlet was passing through the press, *The Westminster Gazette* of November 23, was received. It contains a full account of an "Order" by Mr. Judge, containing the following charges against her, and ending with her Deposition, all under Mahatmic authority!

Insincerity.—"While she was writing to me most kindly and working with me, she was all the time thinking that I was a forger and that I had blasphemed the Master. She was made to conceal from me when here, her thoughts about the intended charges, but was made to tell Mr. Keightly, in London, and possibly a few others. Nor until the time was ripe did she tell me, in her letter, in January, from India, asking me to resign from the E. S. T. and the T. S. offices, saying that if I did and would confess guilt, all would be forgiven, and every one would work with me as usual. But I was directed differently, and fully informed. She was induced to believe that the Master was endorsing the prosecution, that he was ordering her to do what she did."

Black Magic.—"She (Mrs. Besant) felt and expressed to me the greatest pain to have to do such things to me. I knew she so felt, and wrote her that it was the Black Magicians.

"The plot exists among the Black Magicians, who ever war against the White, and against those Black ones we were constantly warned by H. P. B. This is no fiction, but a very substantial fact. I have seen and also been shown the chief entity among those who thus work against us.

"The name of the person who has worked upon so as to, if possible, use him as a minor agent of the Black Magicians, and for the influencing of Mrs. Besant, is Gyanendra N. Chakravarti a Brahman of Allahabad, India, who came to America on our invitation to the Religious Parliament in 1893. He was then a Chela of a minor Indian Guru, and was directed to come to America by that Guru, who had been impressed to so direct him by our Master."

Failure of Mrs. Besant's Magic.—"Her influencers also made her try psychic experiments on me and on two others in Europe. They failed.

---

* *Westminster Gazette*, Nov. 8, 1894.

On me, they had but a passing effect as I was cognisant of them; on one of the others they reflected on health, although she did not desire any harm at all; she was made to think it best and for my good. She then sent word to these persons that she had not succeeded."

Deposition.—"E. S. T. Order, dated November 3."

"I now proceed a step further than the E. S. T. decisions of 1894, and solely for the good of the E. S. T. I resume in the E. S. T. in full, all the functions and powers given to me by H. P. B., and that came to me by orderly succession after her passing from this life, and declare myself the sole head of the E. S. T. This has been done already in America. So far as concerns the rest of the E. S. T., I may have to await the action of the members, but I stand ready to exercise those functions in every part of it. Hence under the authority given me by the Master and H. P. B., and under Master's direction, I declare Mrs. Annie Besant's headship in the E. S. T., at an end."

(Signed) *William Q. Judge.*

TRUE STATEMENT OF THE CASE BY MR. JUDGE.

"Now then, either I am bringing you a true message from the Master, or the whole T. S. and E. S. T., is a lie, in the ruins of which must be buried the names of H. P. B. and the Masters. All these stand together as they fall together."

No one except an "imbecile" can hesitate a moment which alternative to adopt.

THEOSOPHY, A RETURN TO EXPLODED SUPERSTITIONS OF THE MIDDLE AGES.

The Indian Magazine, edited by Miss Manning, and the organ of the Indian Association, is well-known and esteemed by intelligent Hindus, and cannot be charged with a Missionary bias. A recent article shows that the movement has not assisted but opposed Indian progress in every respect, seeking to revive exploded superstitions. This is pointed out in the following extracts:

Theosophists are fond of assuming that they represent a movement which is serviceable to the true interests of the natives of India. They also assert that the Theosophical Society " promotes the study of Aryan, and other Eastern literatures, religions, and sciences."

Let us see how far these fair sounding professions are in agreement with the performances of those who make them. And, first of all, in what way does the Theosophical movement serve Indian interests? It is true, Theosophists —following the example of their founder, Madame Blavatsky—have many agreeable and flattering things to say about Eastern civilisations generally, and especially about the civilisation of ancient India; and that they say many disagreeable and contemptuous things about Western civilisations, and about the civilisation of modern England in particular. But, then, to praise ancient India, and to abuse modern England, does not establish a claim to serve the interests of the Indian people. The tendency of these extravagant flatteries of Eastern customs and views of life, on the one hand, and of the exaggerated abuse of Western customs and views of life, on the other, is to strengthen Eastern exclusiveness, and to embitter race antipathies; and such an influence is not serviceable, but injurious, to the advancement of India in the present day.

I suppose we may take as the most competent judges of what is really advantageous to the interests of the native community, those patriotic Indians who have devoted themselves to the educational, social, and political progress of their country. We find these leaders of Indian progress not assisted, but opposed, by the influences of Theosophy. Theosophists would have young Indians believe that their own literatures contain all wisdom and knowledge, and that they can only derive error and impiety from Western sources. On the contrary, many distinguished Indians, belonging to the Mohammedan, Hindu, and Parsee communities, are agreed in desiring that native students should have the benefit of Western practical training and scientific education to qualify them to become actively useful to their country. They also agree in urging upon young Indians, whose means admit of it, that they should travel, and acquaint themselves with Western methods of thought and habits of life. Certainly, patriotic native gentlemen, who themselves continue to hold the religious faiths of their ancestors, are not in favour of any renunciation on the part of the younger generation, of the spiritual beliefs belonging to the creeds in which they were born. But the influence of these enlightened men is used to help their compatriots to distinguish between spiritual beliefs and mischievous and degrading superstition; and to convince them that irrational and inhuman practices are opposed to the purposes that their own prophets and teachers had in view. Theosophists, on the contrary, insist upon the sacred authority of these superstitions. They defend, by the mouths of their chief representatives—Madame Blavatsky, Colonel Olcott, and Mrs. Besant—the very institutions and practices that enlightened Indians most deplore: the institution of caste; the unlimited privileges of the Brahmans; the servitude and seclusion of women; the worship of idols; the belief in charms, exorcisms, and incantations; the terror of sorcery; the hideous self-macerations and mutilations of yogee-ism; the fanatical perversion that leads persons capable of sacrifice to waste their devotion in inflicting aimless torments upon themselves, instead of in conferring benefits upon their fellow-creatures, &c. In the opinion of Madame Blavatsky and Mrs. Besant, it is in the restoration of such practices, and in a general revival of enthusiasm for ancient Sanskrit literature, and their old religions and philosophies—properly explained and added to by Theosophists—that the future hope of the Indian people must be found. In the opinion of practical Indian reformers, this hope lies in the emancipation of their compatriots from superstition; and in their deliverance from those prejudices that create divisions between men of different creeds and castes, and prevent them working together for the social and political interests they have in common. As for early Sanskrit literature, and old Indian philosophy and religious thought, it is not probable that Theosophists either understand their value better, or take more delight and pride in their special beauties, than do the direct heirs of the original creators of these treasures. At the same time, enthusiasm for Sanskrit literature, and a renewal of zeal for philosophical and religious speculations, are not the passions that Indian leaders of progress desire to see just now stimulated in the minds of their contemporaries; they recognise that if these subjects have not in the past occupied their countrymen too much, the economic, social, and political welfare of their native land has interested them too little. They now desire to awaken a sense of obligations in young Indians to occupy themselves with the more practical aspects of life, fit themselves for actively useful careers.

In all these directions, then, the influences of Theosophy are opposed to the interests of the natives of India. And this opposition is not the result of an accidental misunderstanding on the part of the founders of Theosophy as to what these real interests actually are. It must be borne in mind that in India, as in Europe and America, the founders and leaders of Theosophy have pursued, and still continue to pursue, one object; and that all other professed aims, social, religious, or humanitarian, they may claim to serve by the way, are merely put forward to assist, or to screen, this supreme object. The Object consistently pursued by Theosophic leaders is the re-establishment of the belief in magic and witchcraft, the dethronement of intelligence, and the restoration of the old dominion of superstition over the human mind. In the pursuit of this end, it is inevitable that Theosophy, wherever it may strike roots, should find itself in antagonism to all movements that have enlightenment, emancipation, and progress for their aims. Occultists, and the monopolists of secret doctrines, are not likely to approve of the spread of popular education, and the open investigations of science. Theurgists, and revivers of magical processes, are bound to affect scorn of reason and of the intellectual culture that condemn them. Dogmatists, who make a primæval revelation the standard of truth and virtue, necessarily undervalue the authority of the moral sense, and the worth of knowledge obtained by methods of observation and thought. Defenders of the privileges and superiority of a sacred caste, compared with whom mankind at large is described as the "common herd," and the "masses of the profane," are, whatever may be their professions, incapable of feeling or teaching the doctrine of Human Brotherhood that has its foundation upon principles of equality and justice, and upon the sentiment of the native dignity of man....

Again, the "philosophy" as preached by the "Masters" is not "a grand and beneficent philosophy" upon its own merits: but the reverse. The effort to revive the belief in magic and the terror of sorcery is a conspiracy against the intelligence of the age. The endeavour to restore dogmatic authority, and the spiritual supremacy of a priestly caste, is an effort to recall the most mischievous tyrannies that have held the human mind and conscience in bondage. The discouraging doctrine that wisdom and human perfection lie behind us in the unrecoverable past, not before us in the attainable future, is a denial of all that lends ideal faith and hope to the noblest movements of our day. The encouragement of personal vanity in their defects of health and judgment on the part of persons of imperfectly balanced mind, and hysterical temperament, is injurious to the cultivation of habits of self-control and of intellectual discipline, the safeguard necessary to restrain these personages from becoming infected themselves, and the means of infecting others, with insanity. These and other peculiarities that are characteristic of the "philosophy" preached by, or for, the Masters, make the so-called philosophy a demoralising and humiliating disease, that distorts all it touches, and disfigures every subject with which it deals."

There is an elaborate work, by P. Lacroix, on the *Science and Literature of the Middle Ages*.* One of the Chapters is on "The Occult Sciences." The following are some of them; Oneiromancy, (divining of dreams) astrology, chiromancy, palmistry (divining by the hand) magic, necromancy (revealing future events through the dead), &c.

A "List of Theosophical Books to be obtained at the Theosophist Office, Adyar, Madras," has been published. An Adver-

---

* Bickers, publisher.

tisement in *The Hindu*, after giving a selection from it, adds, " And 500 more works upon Religion, Magic, Sorcery, Phantoms, Spiritualism, Thought-Reading, Psychometry, Astrology, Palmistry, Hygienic, &c.

The following are some of the titles with their explanations:

	Rs.	A.
Magic, White and Black, by Dr. F. Hartmann	1	12
Very popular treatise upon Magic.		
Occult Sciences, by A. E. Waite	5	0
An account of magical practices.		
Bible in India by Louis Jacolliot*	9	0
Hindu origin of Hebrew and Christian Revelation.		
The Debatable Land between the World and the Next, by Owen..	6	0
Touching communication of religious knowledge to men, with illustrative narratives.		
Posthumous Humanity, by M. D. Assier, and Colonel Olcott	5	8
A most interesting work on astral phantoms, very suggestive to Hindus especially.		
Planchette Mystery	0	10
The Medium's Book, Experimental Spiritism	6	0
Chiromancy, by Firth and Heron-Allen	0	12
A concise exposition of how to read and to foretell events.		
Manual of Cheirosophy, by E. H. Allen (the best book on Palmistry)	4	0
Grammar of Palmistry, by Katherine St. Hill	1	0
[All the above are useful books.]		
Book of Dreams, by Raphael	0	12
Text Book of Astrology, by A. J. Pearse, 2 Vols.	18	0
Astrology—a Series of four Lectures, by W. R. Old	0	8
Key to Astrology, by Raphael	0	13
Geomancy, by F. Hartmann	1	14
The art of divining by punctuation.		
Hand-book of Cartomancy, by Grand Orient	1	12
(The art of telling fortunes with cards. *Webster*.)		
History of Magic, by J. Ennemoser (2 Vols. Highly recommended)	9	0
A repository of very important facts.		
Mysteries of Magic, by A. E. Waite	9	0
Translation of a famous work by Eliphas Levi.		
Fascination, or the Philosophy of Charming	3	2

There is a monthly magazine, called *The Theosophist*, published in Madras, commenced by Madame Blavatsky. The *Saturday Review* thus characterised its contents when under her management:

"*The Theosophist* is full of translations from the works of ancient 'theurgists,' of 'spirit communications,' and of blatant nonsense of all kinds, flavoured with the pseudo-science and second-hand archæology which distinguish 'trance lecturos' and the utterances of 'materialized spirits.' Our

---

* The worthless character of this book has been exposed by Max Müller, but it was a great authority with Madame Blavatsky.

old friend Zadkiel, too, has a good word said for him. '*Omne ignotum pro magnifico*" is a trite adage; and we dare say that all this rubbish presents itself to the Hindu mind as serious Western lore.

"A clumsy attempt has been made to spread the false and pernicious doctrines of 'Spiritualism' among the too impressionable inhabitants of India, and to bolster up the balderdash with pseudo-oriental learning which will not bear for one moment the test of scholarly criticism."*

It fully maintains the above reputation under Colonel Olcott's editorship. The following specimens are culled from a single issue, November, 1894.

In an article on "Clairvoyance and the Phenomena of the Double," the following remarkable facts are mentioned:

"A further characteristic of clairvoyance, when associated with the projection of the double, seems to be indicated when the seer falls into a lifeless condition, which may be connected with a partial diversion of the life principle, and is, at the same time, seen at a distant place." p. 78.

"Remigins relates: A French merchant who had travelled into Italy, wanted to get news of his home through a conjurer. He was made to wait an hour in the adjoining room and was then told that his younger brother was dead, his wife delivered of twins, and servant had stolen a bag of money, all of which proved correct." p. 79.

"A similar case is given by Bodin: "In the year 1546, when I was at Nantes, I heard of seven sorcerers, who said in the hearing of several persons, that within an hour they would bring news of all that was taking place ten miles around. Thereupon they fell into a kind of swoon, and remained in this position full three hours. Then they stood up and said what they had seen in the town of Nantes and roundabout, and wherever they had distinctly perceived the circumstances, places, actions and persons. What they said was found to be true." pp. 79, 80.

"HAUNTED TREES AND STONES."

"Many stories, apparently well authenticated, are told of deaths and illnesses resulting to individuals who have meddled with, or cut down these chosen habitations of the elemental gods." p. 101.

"An English doctor happening to be out on a night case, took refuge under the tree† from a heavy storm that overtook him, while his *saice* handed him his waterproof, holding the pony for him. As the doctor was trying to put on the coat, he suddenly received a blow between the shoulders which nearly felled him to the ground. He thought for a moment that he had been struck by lightning, but then he remembered that there had been no flash. He turned quickly round, but there was nothing to be seen, and to this day he believes that he was struck by some superhuman agency." p. 101.

"A European (lady), who was interested in Spiritualism, wishing to get *en rapport* with the spirit of a certain tree which was commonly reported to be haunted, took a branch of the tree home, and sitting down to a *séance* invoked the said spirit. To her then appeared a headless man who made signs or gave her to understand that he would come the next day with his head if she would do certain things. Terrified out of her senses, the lady brought the *séance* to an abrupt termination." p. 102.

The above may well be described as "balderdash." An intelligent Hindu in Madras observed, that, so far as the influence of Theosophy extended, it had "PUT BACK INDIA HALF A CENTURY."

---

* Quoted in *Bombay Gazette*, Sept. 28, 1881. † One of the above.

THE GREAT MAHATMA HOAX.*

IMPORTANCE OF MAHATMAS.

The Secret Doctrine, of Madame Blavatsky, is professedly founded on revelations through the Mahatmas; the course of the Society has been guided by them. Well, therefore, may Mrs. Besant say:

"**If there are no Mahatmas, the Theosophical Society is an Absurdity.**" *Lucifer*, Dec. 15, 1890.

Mr. Judge, the American Vice-President of the Society, is equally decided on this point (See p. 60). If the message from his Mahatma is a myth, the names of H. P. B. and the Masters must be buried in the ruins of the Society.

NATURE OF MAHATMAS.

During her recent Australian tour, Mrs. Besant gave a lecture on Mahatmas, of which the following abstract is given in the *Westminster Gazette* of November 6, 1894:—

The Australian mail, which has just arrived in London, brings an account of a lecture delivered by Mrs. Besant in the Sydney Opera House, on September 28 to a crowded audience. Mrs. Besant commenced by informing her hearers that she had met Mahatmas, but she did not enter into details. She dealt, however, upon the superhuman nobleness, purity, and power of these spirits. They needed, however, no defence from her. It was not for their sakes, but for the sake of mankind, that she spoke to the world at large.

MAHATMAS AS "DIVINE MEN."

First as to what Mahatmas were. A Mahatma was a man living in a human body, who, in the course of evolution by means of repeated incarnations, had reached the highest possible point of human perfection—physically, intellectually, and morally; a man who had acquired all the powers of the human soul, and had acquired all the knowledge to be found on earth—literally a Divine man. Mahatmas had always possessed superhuman powers. They were able, indeed, to control the powers of Nature.

THE EVIDENCE OF THEIR EXISTENCE.

Coming to the evidence for the existence of Mahatmas at the present day, Mrs. Besant pointed out that the only possible evidence of the existence of people at a distance was human testimony. That evidence they possessed by the testimony of a number of honourable and credible people who had come into personal contact with them. There was Madame Blavatsky, Colonel Olcott, and so on—man after man, and woman after woman, who had testified to having personally seen them. Madame Blavatsky had been taught by a Mahatma who had come specially to London for that purpose. Mrs. Besant said that she herself could add her own personal testimony of the fact of their existence, and if anyone challenged to her the existence of these teachers it was just as if they challenged the existence of some intimate friend of hers in London.

---

* An *Exposé* under this title is to be issued by *the Westminster Gazette*.

How to become a Mahatma.

The question of the existence of Mahatmas having been settled by this and other arguments, Mrs. Besant proceeded to describe how Mahatmas were evolved. If a man wished to become a disciple, and so ultimately a Mahatma, he had to obey certain rules. He must study for twelve, twenty-four, or thirty-six years, and then he had to pass into the life of a householder and rear a family. This was always a part of the discipline and training of an aspirant to Mahatmaship. Having attained as near moral perfection as he could by the practice of virtues, the next step for the disciple was to die and be reincarnated again and again without any prolonged rest in Paradise between the incarnations. All this time the Mahatmas would be teaching and guiding him until he reached perfection, and the infinite bliss of Paradise lay before him. Then came the great renunciation made by all Mahatmas. Instead of entering Paradise he would turn back and say he would never cross the threshold till all men crossed it with him and all sorrow was at an end. He would turn back to be one of the helpers of humanity, one of the bearers of the burden of the world, and that was the Mahatma. (Loud cheers.)

How to know a Mahatma when you see Him.

Mahatmas did from time to time come among men. One of the brethren was in London in 1851 for a special purpose, but none of them had been recognised, for they had nothing to distinguish them save their dignity and silence. It was only when the soul was awakened that a Mahatma could be recognised, and then it was not necessary to meet them in the physical body. The awakened soul could communicate with them at a distance. Another reason why they did not come among men was that it was a great waste of spiritual force for them to come amongst the "befouled magnetism" of men in Western civilisation. "If a Mahatma came to Sydney he would be poisoned by the mere exhalations of the foulness through which he would have to pass, unless he exercised a great power of flinging from him all this foul matter, and so preserved his own magnetism pure, no matter how foul the surroundings." (Great applause.)

The Quaternion of Witnesses for the Existence of Mahatmas.

Indubitable evidence is required to show that such exalted personages are not a myth. Mrs. Besant affirmed that the "evidence they possessed was the testimony of a number of honourable and credible people, who had come into personal contact with them. There was Madame Blavatsky, Colonel Olcott, and so on—man after man, and woman after woman, who had testified to having personally seen them." She modestly did not mention herself, although she told the Tanjore correspondent of the *Madras Mail* that she had seen one. (See page 46). To these may be added Mr. Judge, the Mahatmic postmaster in succession to Madame Blavatsky.

Let these "honourable and credible people" be examined in turn :

I. **Madame Blavatsky.**—Mrs. Besant admits that if the "phenomena," were not true, Madame Blavatsky was *a miserable impostor, an accomplice of tricksters, a foul and loathsome deceiver,* *a conjurer with trap doors and sliding panels.*" That she was an "impostor" is proved by what Professor Sidgwick considers "irresistible" evidence. (see page 35.)

Madame Blavatsky's conduct is the worse, as she hypocritically expressed the highest admiration of *truth.* The motto of *The Theosophist,* which she edited, was, "There is no Religion higher than Truth;" the "moral standard of *The Theosophist,* is TRUTH." A Theosophist banner had the inscription, "There is no Duty higher than Truth."

II. **Colonel Olcott.**—This gentleman, Professor Sidgwick says in his Report, showed "extraordinary credulity and inaccuracy in observation and inference." This is most abundantly confirmed by his own volume, *People from the Other World* (See pp. 5, 6). For a man who has seen "more than 500 apparitions of dead persons," acquaintance with "15 Mahatmas" is no great wonder. Dr. Daly, his quondam associate, describes him as a "theorist of very shallow understanding, and colossal vanity."*

III. **Mrs. Besant.**—The value of this lady's testimony will be examined more in detail. It is worth little for the following reasons:

(1) *Her inability to weigh evidence.* Take the case of Madame Blavatsky. The evidence that she was an impostor was the following:—

1. Seventy or eighty of her own letters, including a number professedly written by Mahatmas. Madame Blavatsky asserted that these letters were forgeries, in whole or in part; but when challenged to prove this in a court of law, she prudently declined.

2. The evidence of A. O. HUME, ESQ., in whose house Madame Blavatsky resided for some months, and to whom several Mahatma letters were addressed.†

3. The investigation by the Editor of the *Madras Christian College Magazine,* confirmed by Dr. Miller and the Professors of the Madras Christian College.

4. The Report of the Psychical Research Society, written by Professor Sidgwick, of Cambridge, after the receipt of Mr. Hodgson's Account of his Investigations. Mr. Hodgson, a Cambridge graduate, spent three months in India inquiring into the evidence for the alleged "phenomena."

One would have thought that such charges, supported by such evidence, would have been long and carefully investigated by Mrs. Besant; but after reading Professor Sidgwick's Report she "flung it aside with righteous scorn," and within 24 hours became a member of the Theosophical Society.

What was it that apparently weighed most with her in coming to such a decision?

---

* *Indian Daily News,* Oct. 1, 1894.
† See *Proceedings of the Psychical Research Society,* December 1885, p. 274.

"*The proud fiery truthfulness that shone at me from the clear blue eyes—honest and fearless as those of a noble child.*"

Such evidence may be deemed sufficient by a woman to refute any amount of testimony on the other side; but lawyers will rate it at its proper value. They prefer looking to scores of letters rather than to "clear blue eyes."

2. *Her frequent changes of opinion.*—She has been well described in the words:

> "*Stiff in opinions, always in the wrong,
> Everything by starts, and nothing long.*"

Stiff in Opinion.—Mr. Foote, her free-thought fellow-worker, remarked that in all Mrs. Besant's changes, she remained "quite positive."

In this world of sin and sorrow, the greatest comfort a sufferer can have is to believe that however sore his affliction, it all proceeds from the loving hand of a heavenly Father, intended to work for good in the end. When loved ones are taken away by death, how consoling it is to look forward to a world where death and separation are unknown, where parent and child, husband and wife, dwell for ever together in happiness.

When Mrs. Besant embraced atheism and materialism, she went about doing her utmost to rob people of these solaces, proudly putting her opinion against the conclusions of the greatest and wisest men in all ages.

The "Path to Atheism" was described as being in the end "fragrant with all the flowers of summer;" the golden age of the world was to be restored when man was seated on "the usurped throne of God!"

She is now equally "positive" with regard to the beneficial results of Theosophy. She hopes that

> "The tale of one soul that went out alone into the darkness and on the other side found light, that struggled through the storm and found peace, may bring some ray of light and peace into the darkness and storm of other lives."

The Kural, a famous South Indian poem, says, "All lights are not *true* lights." Mrs. Besant's light is only a beacon of warning.

"*Always in the Wrong.*"—Mrs. Besant professes to be an earnest seeker after truth. She asks for no other epitaph upon her tomb than

"She tried to follow Truth."

Notwithstanding this, it has been her unhappy lot to devote most of her adult life to the zealous propagation of deadly errors, and to choose as her Guru a consummate hypocrite. The following are some illustrations of her being "in the wrong" at one period or another in her history:

Truth.	Mrs. Besant on the side of Error.
Theism.	Atheism.
Man has a Soul.	Materialism.
A Future State.	Death ends All.
Belief in Prayer.	Prayer a Contradiction.
The Pardon of Sin.	Karma Unchangeable.
The Need of Divine Help.	Man his own Saviour.
Monotheism.	Pantheism and Polytheism.
Idolatry forbidden.	"Preserve your Idols."
The Brotherhood of Man.	"Keep your Caste Marks."
Progress the idea of Civilization.	Hindu Civilization the oldest and best in the World.
A fiction of Madame Blavatsky.	Belief in the "Seven Kosmic Planes," &c.
Madame Blavatsky proved, by "irresistible" evidence to be an "impostor."	The evidence "flung aside with righteous scorn," and Madame Blavatsky acknowledged as the world's "Great Teacher."

"*Everything by starts, and nothing long.*"—In her many changes of belief Mrs. Besant has been fitly compared to a stage player, who suddenly retreats behind the scenes, and re-appears in a different character. She has been PROTESTANT and HIGH CHURCH CHRISTIAN, ANTI-CHRISTIAN, THEIST, ATHEIST, MATERIALIST, ANTI-MATERIALIST, MALTHUSIAN, ANTI-MALTHUSIAN, SPIRITUALIST, THEOSOPHIST, PANTHEIST, POLYTHEIST, HINDU.

Her friend Mr. Stead thinks that her changes are not yet over. He says "the prediction was made long ago that Mrs. Besant would die in the odour of sanctity within the pale of the Catholic Church."

3. *Her Self-Confidence.*—A celebrated Greek philosopher in ancient times said: "Atheism is a disease of the soul before it becomes an error of the understanding." The "disease" of Mrs. Besant's soul is pride. Madame Blavatsky, whom she calls her "Guru," saw through her character: "Child, your pride is terrible; you are as proud as Lucifer himself."*

It has been shown that Madame Blavatsky was a charlatan, making claims to knowledge which she did not possess. This is proved by her calling the Bhagavad Gita the "Bagaved gitta," and by the assertion that "Maha Maya or Maha Deva was the mother of Bhudda!" Her "*Secret Doctrine*" is a mystical jumble of baseless speculations, derived from comparatively modern European works, though professed to be obtained from Mahatmas. Babu Brajendranath Seal, in letters to *The Indian Messenger*, shows "Mrs. Besant's inability to comprehend the recent discoveries of

---

* *Borderland*, Oct. 1893, p. 175.

science, and her hazy notions about Hindu philosophy" notwithstanding "her pompous claims to first-hand scientific knowledge and her implied access to the teachings of the Hindu Shastras and Darsanas."*

* Mrs. Besant's "seven Kosmic planes of manifestation," "the seven globes in a planetary chain," "the seven races on each planet," &c. are accepted on the authority of imaginary Mahatmas, proved to be plagiarists and liars. *The Indian Magazine* justly says :

"If dishonest people whom we know to have been guilty of falsehood and trickery in this present state of existence choose to dogmatise about the condition of life in other spheres, we are justified in rejecting their statements off hand; for, if they are not to be believed concerning things that can be seen, how are we to believe them when they prophesy about the unseen?"

The Times quotes the following as describing Theosophical speculations : "talking grave nonsense on subjects beyond the reach of the human understanding."

MR. GLADSTONE thus refers to Mrs. Besant in *The Nineteenth Century*, when noticing her *Autobiography* :

"Her readers will find, that the book is a spiritual itinerary, and that it shows with how much at least of intellectual ease, and what unquestioning assumptions of being right, vast spaces of mental travelling may be performed. The stages are, indeed, glaringly in contrast with one another; yet the violent contrarieties do not seem at any period to suggest to the writer so much as a doubt whether the mind which so continually changes in attitude and colour can after all be very trustworthy in each and all its movements. This uncomfortable suggestion is never permitted to intrude; and the absolute self-complacency of the authoress bears her through tracts of air buoyant and capacious enough to carry the Dircean swan. Mrs. Besant passes from her earliest to her latest stage of thought as lightly, as the swallow skims the surface of the lawn, and with just as little effort to ascertain what lies beneath it. An ordinary mind would suppose that modesty was the one lesson which she could not have failed to learn from her extraordinary permutations; but the chemist who shall analyse by percentages the contents of these pages will not, I apprehend, be in a condition to report that of such an element he can find even the infinitesimal quantity usually and conveniently denominated a 'trace.' Her several schemes of belief or non-belief appear to have been entertained one after another, with the same undoubting confidence, until the junctures successively arrived for their not regretful, but rather contemptuous rejection. They are nowhere based upon reasoning, but they rest upon one and the same authority—the authority of Mrs. Besant."

Among other remarks the following may be quoted :

"She is sensible of having been much governed by vanity at that period of her life (early childhood), while she does not inform us whether this quality spontaneously disappeared, or what had become of it in the later stages."

"In all her different phases of thought, that place in the mind where the sense of sin should be, appears to have remained, all through the shifting scenes of her mental history, an absolute blank."

---

* *Indian Messenger,* February 18, 1894.

"Speaking generally, it may be held that she has followed at times her own impulsions with an entire sincerity; but that those impulsions have been woefully dislocated in origin, spirit, and direction, by an amount of egregious self-confidence which is in itself a guarantee of failure in mental investigation." September, 1894, pp. 317-319.

MR. GARRETT, author of the articles in *The Westminster Gazette*, possessed special advantages for forming an opinion as he had in his possession attested copies of the suppressed evidence against Mr. Judge. What does he think of her?

"Mrs. Besant has been bamboozled for years by bogus 'communications' of the most childish kind, and in so ludicrous a fashion as to deprive of all value any future evidence of hers on any question calling for the smallest exercise of observation and common sense.

"She would in all probability be firmly believing in the bogus documents in question to this day, but for the growing and at last irresistible protests of some less greedily gullible Theosophists.

"That the bamboozling in question has been practised widely and systematically, ever since Madame Blavatsky's death, pretty much as it used to be during her lifetime.

"That official acts of the Society, as well as those of individual members, have been guided by these bogus messages from Mahatmas.

"That the exposure of them leaves the Society absolutely destitute of any objective communications with the Mahatmas who are alleged to have founded and to watch over it, and of all other evidence of their existence.

"That Mrs. Besant has taken a leading part in hushing up the facts of this exposure, and so securing the person whom she believes to have written the bogus documents in his tenure of the highest office but one of the Society.

"And that therefore Mrs. Besant herself and all her colleagues are in so far in the position of condoning the hoax, and are benefiting in one sense or another by the popular delusion which they have helped to propagate."*

IV. **Mr. Judge.**—The facts mentioned prove incontestibly that the American head of the Society was guilty of lying and fraud. He produced "bogus," messages, alleged to have been sent by "Mahatma Morya" and attested by his seal, the history of which has been given.

Such are the "honourable and credible witnesses" for

"**The Great Mahatma Hoax.**"

---

* *The Westminister Gazette*, October, 29, 1894.

MADAME BLAVATSKY'S CONTEMPT FOR HER DUPES.

Madame Blavatsky secretly ridiculed those whom she deceived. They were characterised as "domestic imbeciles," "familiar muffs."

But Madame Blavatsky's greatest scorn was reserved for Colonel Olcott, who so much assisted her in establishing the Society. As already mentioned, he was called a "psychologised baby," who "did not know his head from his heels;" "flapdoodle (food for fools) Olcott," " an idiot."

It would be interesting to know what she thought of Mrs. Besant. Very probably, *mutatis mutandis* (with the necessary changes), what she wrote about Colonel Olcott:

"The Yankees thought themselves very smart, and Colonel Olcott thought he was particularly smart, even for a Yankee, but he would have to get up much earlier in the morning to be as smart as she was."*

The *Bombay Gazette's* estimate of Theosophist intellect is not much more flattering than that of Madame Blavatsky. Referring to Mr. Sinnett, author of *The Occult World*, it is said:

"We have to face the unpleasant fact that the author and one or two others who, like himself, had some claim to be accepted as representatives here of European learning and culture, have subscribed their faith to as ridiculous a scheme of things as ever called itself a philosophy, and that they have done so on the evidence of as patent a series of juggling tricks as ever imposed on the bumpkins at a village fair." Sept. 24th, 1881.

The *New York Herald*, referring to Mr. A. P. Sinnett, says that he "brays with a fatuous ingenuousness and with a good faith that are charming and purely asinine."

Mr. Garrett says:

"Till May, 1891, Madame was the principal witness to the objective existence and attributes of Mahatmas. Since that date the principal witness is William Q. Judge."

In July, 1894, a circular was issued, signed by Colonel Olcott, A. P. Sinnett, Mrs. Besant, Bertram Keightly, and others, dwelling on the importance of *truth*. "We must love truth, seek truth, and live truth." Why was the issue of such a circular necessary? Was it not elicited by the Mahatmic seal? was it not a homily intended for the special benefit of W. Q. Judge?

Mr. Garrett suggests that the "faithful," when they file into the Occult Room at the next convention to gaze through peep holes at the two August Portraits of Mahatmas, should have the courage to ask their officials plainly what evidence they can now offer that either of the subjects of those fancy portraits ever existed.†

---

* *Proceedings of Psychical Research Society*, Dec. 1885, p. 310.
† *Westminster Gazette*, November 8th, 1894.

Mrs. Besant admits that the "only possible evidence" of the existence of Mahatmas is "human testimony" (page 65). It has been shown that there is not a shred of this of a credible character. Mr. H. Burrows scouts the need of testimony. Like the Germans, he evolves Mahatmas out of the "depths of his inner consciousness." Replying to a newspaper representative he said:—

"My general position with regard to Mahatmas is, that as an evolutionist, I believe in the development and progress not merely of the body, but also of the soul. A Mahatma—literally 'great soul'—is a human being who, by long physical, mental and moral training, has attained to more knowledge of the universe and its really vital forces than the ordinary person. The belief in the existence of any particular Mahatma must depend upon the personal experience of the student. I believe, this is impregnable scientific ground, and on it I take my stand."*

The whole history of the Theosophic movement, from the time that Madame Blavatsky duped Colonel Olcott at the farm of the Eddy Brothers, to the Mahatmic seal and deposition of Mrs. Besant, is a sickening record of fraud on the one hand, and "voracious credulity" on the other. The revelations of the *Westminster Gazette* will open the eyes of some; but so great is human folly, that a tolerably full gathering of "imbeciles," "muffs", and "babies" may nevertheless be expected at the Adyar.

"A CORRUPT TREE BRINGETH FORTH EVIL FRUIT."

The "Great Teacher" says: "Do men gather grapes of thorns or figs of thistles?" What was the character of the founder of the "Wisdom Religion?"

She was notoriously irascible; but her fatal defect was want of truthfulness.

Hints on Esoteric Philosophy, No. I., a pamphlet published during her lifetime, "Issued under the Authority of the Theosophical Society," and acknowledged by Mr. A. O. Hume, contains the following:

"Madame Blavatsky's converse is..... too often replete with contradictions, inaccuracies, and at times apparently distinct misstatements. . . .

"Her memory is undoubtedly impaired, and not unfrequently, I believe, she quite *unconsciously*, in the course of conversation, makes incorrect, if not absolutely false, statements." pp. 68, 69.

The charge of lying is not confined to individual cases; she is accused of "*consciously weaving for years an enormous network of falsehood.*" The case is thus stated by Mr. Sinnett:—

"There is no immediate alternative between the conclusion that her statements concerning the Brothers are broadly true, and the conclusion that she is what some American enemies have called her, 'the champion impostor

---

* Quoted in *The Hindu*, Dec. 15, 1894.

of the age.' ... Either she must be right, or she has consciously been weaving an enormous network of falsehood in all her writings, acts, and conversation for the last eight or nine years. ... Pare away as much as you like from the details of Madame Blavatsky's statement on account of possible exaggeration, and that which remains is a great solid block of residual statement which must be either true, or a structure of conscious falsehood."*

The "imbeciles" and the world differ as to the alternative to be accepted.

Combination of Scepticism and Credulity in Theosophists.— Persons who are too wise to believe in the existence of an intelligent Creator, accept as true the grossest absurdities. This is nothing new. Lecky says in his *History of European Morals* :—

"There existed, too, to a very large extent, a kind of superstitious scepticism which occupies a very prominent place in religious history." Vol. I. p. 179.

"The period when Roman incredulity reached its extreme point had been the century that preceded and the half century that followed the birth of Christ ..... This disbelief, however, as I have already noticed, co-existed with numerous magical and astrological superstitions." *Ibid*, p. 330.

"The notions, too, of magic and astrology, were detached from all theological belief, and might be found among many who were absolute atheists." *Ibid*, p. 393.

The Society, as such, does not profess to have any theological creed ; but its founders are avowed atheists. Theists do not understand by a " personal God," a Being with a body ; but one conscious of His own existence, and acting with intelligence. " Personal " is introduced to distinguish it from a mere force, like gravitation.

Madame Blavatsky, in reviewing *The Theosophical Society*, by the Rev. A. Theophilus, makes the confession :

" Now we desire the reader to properly understand that personally we do not at all deny the charge of atheism, the word being used in an orthodox theistic sense."†

The following statement is admitted to be " correct:" " Colonel Olcott, as well as Madame Blavatsky, told the Pandit in the presence of several respectable gentlemen that they did not at all believe in the existence of God."‡

Colonel Olcott, in a catechism which he compiled in Ceylon, where he professed to be a Buddhist, says :

"A personal god Buddhists regard as only a gigantic shadow thrown upon the void of space by the imagination of ignorant men." No. 112.

The *Bombay Gazette*, reviewing *The Occult World*, by Mr. A. P. Sinnett, a prominent member of the Society, says :—

"The first act of faith required of the disciple of Occult Philosophy is to purge his mind of belief in an imaginary personal God (p. 135) and all simi-

---

* *The Occult World*, pp. 152, 153.
† *The Theosophist* Sept. 1882.
‡ *The Theosophist* June 1882, see p. 7.

lar 'current superstitions,' (p. 139). This, we may say in passing, is not in all cases so difficult as one might suppose. Our author, at least, as we shall see, had so loose a hold on these venerable beliefs, that a trick with a clock shade was enough to dislodge them, one and all, from his mind." Sept. 24, 1881.

Whatever Mrs. Besant may now think, for many years she was an avowed atheist. " I do not believe in a personal God ; the concept is impossible to one."

The above quotations prove *scepticism* ; the whole of the foregoing pages demonstrate *credulity*. The combination is the same as that mentioned by Lecky.

No Prayer.—Colonel Olcott says in his *Addresses* : " The Founders of the Theosophical Society do not pray." (p. 119). They are not illustrations, either intellectually or otherwise, of the advantages of such a course. It must, however, be admitted that they are carrying out their principles logically, for it is useless to pray to a Being who does not exist or to an Entity who is practically a nonentity.

Of the " Wisdom Religion," it may be said, *Hic Deus nihil-fecit* (Here God did nothing). It may well be called *Atheosophy*, godless wisdom, rather than *Theosophy*.

STUDY OF HINDUISM.

While books full of error, like those of Madame Blavatsky, are worse than useless, educated Hindus are recommended to study their own religion through its recognised standards. A beginning should be made with the Vedas, on which it is professedly based. Formerly their contents were almost unknown; copies of the Rig-Veda, the most important, are now easily procurable.

Only a very few Indian scholars are able to understand the Rig-Veda in Sanskrit: an imperfect knowledge of the language is worthless for this purpose. English translations, however, by competent scholars give a fair idea of the original.

There is a translation of the whole work by Professor Wilson and others ; Professor Max Müller has one in progress. The best and cheapest complete translation now available is by Mr. R. T. GRIFFITH, for many years Principal of the Government College, Benares, where he had the assistance of the ablest pandits in India. Valuable explanatory notes are added throughout. It is published by E. J. Lazarus & Co., Benares, Price Rs. 16 in 16 parts ; or Rs. 19-12-0 in 4 volumes.

If possible, the complete translation should be obtained ; but as this is beyond the means of most, a cheap selection has been published.

AN ACCOUNT OF THE VEDAS WITH ILLUSTRATIVE EXTRACTS. 8vo. 166 pp. 4½ As. Post-free, 6 As.

With the kind permission of Mr. Griffith, it contains a few of the most important hymns, in whole or in part, from the ten Mandalas. The first hymn is given in Nagri and Roman character as well as in English. The hymns quoted in full include one addressed by Sunahsepa to Varuna when bound to the sacrificial post, and the celebrated Purusha Sukta hymn.

There are selections from 11 hymns in the Atharva Veda. One of them is regarded as a spell, "To recall from Death." Short extracts from the Aitareya Brahmana and the Satapatha Brahmana give some idea of their character.

There is an Introduction of 66 pages, compiled from the works of Max Müller, Muir, Haug, Whitney, Rajendra Lala Mitra, and others which will be found very useful.

The translation by Mr. Griffith of the SAMA VEDA in one volume (Rs. 4) is already available, and the translation of the ATHARVA VEDA is in progress.

Professor Max Müller's magnificent series of the *Sacred Books of the East* enables all well acquainted with English to acquire a fair knowledge of their contents. They are by eminent men, furnished with the best aids, and who have given years to their study. They also follow "the critical, comparative, and historical method of inquiry," the value of which is shown by Dr. Bhandarkar in his lecture on the subject. The interpretations of Indian pandits and men like the late Dayanand Sarasvati are often absurd.

Next to the Vedas, the study of the *Bhagavad Gita* is especially recommended. It is supposed to represent the loftiest flights of Hindu philosophy. An abstract of the history of Krishna, as given in the Puranas, and an examination of the doctrines of the Gita, based on extracts from Mr. Telang's translation, are given in the pamphlet named below.*

Among other works the *History of Hindu Civilization in Ancient India*, by Mr. Romesh Chunder Dutt, may be mentioned.†

SCIENTIFIC STUDIES.

The Indian mind is dreamy and imaginative. It greatly needs the discipline of scientific study. But the "Occult Sciences," under the guidance of *The Theosophist*, are not what is meant. *The Indian Magazine* thus notices Madame Blavatsky's ideas of science :—

"Madame Blavatsky's methods were theurgical and occult. For such open but laborious methods as those followed by scholars and men of science

---

* KRISHNA AS DESCRIBED IN THE VISHNU PURANA, BHAGAVATA PURANA, AND THE MAHABHARATA, ESPECIALLY THE BHAGAVAD GITA. 8vo. 72 pp. 2½ As. Post-free, 3 As.

† In 3 Volumes, published by Messrs. Thacker, Spink & Co.

she always made it her business to express a profound contempt. In her *Isis Unveiled*, we have her presuming to teach Sir Richard Proctor astronomy; Faraday and Tyndall natural philosophy; Professor Huxley physiology; while she makes fun of that simpleton Sir Isaac Newton, with his stupid belief in the laws of gravity!"

Colonel Olcott is equally convinced of the superiority of the knowledge possessed by Mahatmas. Addressing Parsees he said :—

"I, a Western man, taught in a Western University, and nursed on the traditions of modern civilization, says that Zaratushta knew more about nature than Tyndall does, more about the laws of force than Balfour Stewart, more about the origin of species than Darwin or Hæckel, more about the human mind and its potentialities than Maudsley or Bain. And so did Buddha and some other proficients in Occult Science." *Addresses*, p. 149.

Colonel Olcott pours contempt on the so-called scientific studies of the Indian Universities. The heads of students are "crammed with a terrible lot of poor stuff;" "they are baked dry in the scholastic ovens of Elphinstone College."* He says ;

"The science we have in mind is a far wider, higher, nobler science than that of modern sciolists. Our view extends over the visible and invisible, the familiar and the unfamiliar, the patent and the occult sides of Nature. In short, ours is the Aryan conception of what science can be and should be, and we point to the Aryans of antiquity as its masters and proficients. Young India is a blind creature whose eyes are not yet open, and the nursing mother of its thought is a bedezened goddess, herself blind of one eye, whose name is modern science." pp. 83, 84.

Colonel Olcott directs the students to *whom* to go for the genuine article :—

"Pshaw! Young man of the Bombay University, when you have taken your degree, and learned all your professors can teach you, go to the hermit and recluse of the jungle, and ask *him* to prove to you where to begin your real study of the world into which you have been born." (p. 149).

The exact *spot* where it is to be found is also clearly indicated :—

"If you drag the depths of the ocean of human nature, if you study the laws of your own self, if you turn the eye of intuition to those profounder depths of natural law, where the demiurgic Hindu Brahma manages the correlation of forces and the rhythmic measures of the atoms, and the eternal principle of motion, called by the Hindus Parabrahm, outbreathes and inhales universes,—*there* will the golden key of this Ineffable Knowledge be found." (p. 129.)

Well did Madame Blavatsky characterise Colonel Olcott as a "psychologised baby." Let science be studied, but through textbooks like those prescribed by the Universities.

ANCIENT MONOTHEISM.

Modern Hindus are both pantheists and polytheists. The number of divinities is popularly said to be 33 crores. The pantheism of the Upanishads is sometimes confounded with mono-

---
* *Addresses*, p. 124.

theism, based on the formula from the Chhandogya Upanishad, *ekam evadvitiyam*, "One only without a second." This is a mistake. The real meaning is, not that there is only one God, but that there is no second anything—a totally different doctrine.

* Some Hindus, unacquainted with the Vedas, think that they contain a pure monotheism. Such is not the case. The religion of the Vedas is polytheistic. The gods are usually spoken of as thrice-eleven, with their wives, as the following quotations will show:

In the third Mandala of the Rig-Veda, Hymn 6, verse 10, Agni is thus addressed :

"Bring, with their wives, the gods, the three-and-thirty, after thy godlike nature, and be joyful."

The following invitation is given to the Asvins :—

"Come O Nasatyas, with the thrice eleven gods; come, O ye Asvins to the drinking of the meath." I. 34. 11.

A hymn to the Visvedevas concludes thus :

"O ye eleven gods whose home is heaven, O ye eleven who make earth your dwelling,

Ye who with might, eleven, live in waters, accept this sacrifice, O gods, with pleasure." I. 139. 11.

It will be seen that the gods are reduced in number from 33 crores to 33 with their wives. In Book iv. 9. 9. the gods are mentioned as being much more numerous: "Three hundred, three thousand, thirty and nine gods have worshipped Agni."

But let us go back beyond the Vedas to the time when the Eastern and Western Aryans lived together, somewhere in Central Asia, and we find monotheism. Max Müller says:

"There is a monotheism which precedes the polytheism of the Veda, and even in the invocation of their innumerable gods, the remembrance of a God, one and infinite, breaks through the mist of an idolatrous phraseology, like the blue sky that is hidden by passing clouds."

The Eastern and Western Aryans, the ancestors of the Hindus, Persians, Greeks, Romans, Germans, French and English, were once living together, speaking the same language, and worshipping the same God under the same name—a name which meant Heaven-Father. This is shown by the Sanskrit DYAUSH-PITAR being the same as the Greek ZEUS-PATER, and the Latin JUPITER.

Max Müller well remarks that when the Aryan nations "search for a name for that which is most exalted and yet most dear to every one of us, which expresses both awe and love, the infinite and the finite," they "can but do what their old fathers did, combine the self-same words, and utter once more the primeval

Aryan prayer, Heaven-Father, in that form which will endure for ever, ' Our Father, which art in heaven.' "*

Educated Hindus! go back to the monotheism which Max Müller says "precedes the polytheism of the Veda." Return to the worship of our great Father in heaven.

The True Jagat Guru, or World's Teacher.

The great truth that there is only one God, our Creator, and Father in heaven, was soon forgotten. Men, in their ignorance, worshipped the sun, moon, and stars, and devised gods after their own evil hearts. Thus in the Vedas we have the worship of Surya, Indra, the sender of rain, Agni, fire, &c. After nature worship, deities like Vishnu and Siva were invented.

Even Hinduism teaches that divine interposition is needed to restore righteousness in the world. In the Bhagavad Gita Krishna is represented as saying:

"Whensoever piety languishes, and impiety is in the ascendant, I create myself. I am born age after age, for the protection of the good, for the destruction of evil-doers and the establishment of piety." VI. 7, 8.

It is shown in the pamphlet on Krishna, already mentioned, that the Avatara of Krishna, as related in the Puranas, does not fulfil these conditions. But Christianity presents a *nishkalank* or spotless Avatara.

The following summary has been given of the mere external facts of Christ's life:—

"In the reign of Augustus Cæsar, a man is born into the world, in an obscure province of the Roman Empire. His parents are poor, —his reputed father being an ordinary mechanic. Nothing noticeable occurs either in his infancy or childhood, if we except the visit to Jerusalem, at twelve years of age. His deportment on this occasion is remarkable, no doubt, exhibiting a ripeness and strength of thought above his years, and in advance of the moral intelligence of the times. But still no condition of humanity is transcended; and the light which had flashed for a moment, as far as the world at large is concerned, goes out again in darkness. Another long interval elapses, and manhood is reached; yet all passes without mark, without observable preparation, without a single inch of ground being cleared away for the erection of that mighty platform,—soon to be the scene of transactions which should convulse the world. Suddenly that platform is raised. It comes up, as it were, in a night, —like the gourd over the prophet's head, but not to perish or pass away. Nations flock to the shadow of it. Unbidden and unknown, Jesus comes forth. Without patronage from the rich, without

---

* *Science of Religions*, p. 178.

countenance from the learned, without sympathy from the men of his own nation, he emerges from the deep seclusion of Nazareth,—a friendless artizan prophet, to bear his resistless testimony against superstition, against hypocrisy, against a corrupt priesthood, against all falsehood, and against all sin. He gathers a little band around him,—obscure in station like himself. And having travelled with this handful of disciples over the cities and villages of Palestine, and having, in the course of his journeys, given to them a body of teaching, unsurpassed for the purity of its precepts, and the sublimity of its doctrines, and the augustness of its disclosures,—after a ministry of three short years, and, under a ban of infamy and disgrace, he dies."*

The Gospel of Theosophy and the Gospel of Jesus Christ compared.—Theosophists have adopted the Buddhist doctrine of *Karma*, which teaches that neither in heaven nor in earth can man escape from the consequences of his acts. The Gospel of Theosophy, the "glorious truth," according to Colonel Olcott, to be proclaimed "through a sin-burdened world," is that

"Eternal, immutable law punishes the slightest moral sin as certainly as it does every physical sin; and, that as man creates his own destiny, so *he* must be his own Saviour and Redeemer, and can have no other." *Addresses*, p. 38.

It is admitted that Christianity also teaches the general truth that men must reap as they sow, but it has its limitations. It is a natural law that severe disease should end in death; but a skilful physician intervenes, and the patient may recover. Although, as a general rule, the punishments decreed by law must be inflicted; the sovereign reserves to himself the right of pardoning if he sees sufficient reason.

Karma, according to Buddhists and Theosophists, is somewhat like fate, an unintelligent force to which there can be no appeal; but it is different if the world is governed by God.

Men instinctively believe in the forgiveableness of sin, and instinctively pray for pardon. An earthly king can pardon an offender; why should this prerogative be denied to the King of kings?

It is admitted that the great problem is how to combine mercy and justice. Christianity sees the difficulty, and points out the solution. God, our heavenly Father, seeing that we could not deliver ourselves from the punishment due to sin, has graciously provided a Saviour, the Lord Jesus Christ. Repenting of our sins and seeking forgiveness in His name, it will assuredly be granted.

Among the last words of Buddha to his followers were, *Attasaraná viharatha*, Be your own refuge. Man is to gain

---

* Moore's *The Age and the Gospel*, pp. 71, 72.

salvation by himself and for himself alone. Such also is the teaching of Theosophy.

When any one sincerely tries to overcome his evil desires, he finds that he is, as it were, tied and bound with the chains of his sins, and needs Divine help. Christianity likewise says, "Work out your own salvation with fear and trembling," but Divine help is offered. A Father's hand is held out to deliver us, and hold us up when we are tempted.

TESTIMONIES TO CHRISTIANITY.

A large number of these, from some of the greatest men that have ever lived, will be found in *Testimonies of Great Men to the Bible and Christianity*.* Only a very few can be quoted.

Gladstone, the most distinguished English statesman of the time, says:

"I see that for the last fifteen hundred years Christianity has always marched in the van of all human improvement and civilization, and it has harnessed to its car all that is great and glorious in the human race."

"Christianity continues to be that which it has been heretofore, the great medicine for the diseases of human nature, the great consolation for its sorrows; the great stay to its weakness, the main and only sufficient guide in the wilderness of the world."

Referring to his own personal belief he says:

"All I write, and all I think, and all I hope is based upon the divinity of our Lord, the one central hope of our poor wayward race."

Lecky, in his *History of European Morals*, bears the following testimony to the EFFECTS of Christianity:—

"It was reserved for Christianity to present to the world a character which, through all the changes of eighteen centuries, has inspired the hearts of men with an impassioned love: has shown itself capable of acting on all ages, temperaments, and conditions; has been not only the highest pattern of virtue, but the strongest incentive to its practice; and has exercised so deep an influence, that the simple record of three years of active life has done more to regenerate and soften mankind than all the discussions of philosophers and all the exhortations of moralists."

Macaulay, in a speech in parliament, describes Christianity as:

"That religion which has done so much to promote justice and mercy, and freedom, and arts, and sciences, and good government, and domestic happiness, which has struck off the chains of the slave, which has mitigated the horrors of war, which has raised women from servants and playthings into companions and friends." To discountenance it he says, "is to commit high treason against humanity and civilisation."

He characterises Christianity as:

"Strong in her sublime philosophy" strong in her spotless morality, strong in those internal and external evidences to which the most powerful and comprehensive of human intellects have yielded assent."

---

* Price 1¼ As. Post-free, 2 As. Sold by Mr. A. T. Scott, Book Depôt, Madras.

English and American atheists seek to give educated Hindus the impression that Christianity is decaying in the West. It has never been more vigorous. Indians have proof of this before their eyes. Every aged Hindu knows that missionaries are now far more numerous than they were when he was young. In the United States 17 new churches, on an average, are built every day by one body of Christians alone. Missionaries are sent not merely to India, but to every accessible part of the earth.

A National Religion.

A cry is raised by some educated Hindus for a *National* religion. It is thought degrading to India to have any other religion than her own.

There is no national geography, astronomy, chemistry, geometry, &c. Science is one all the world over. It is the same with religion. If each country had its own God, there might be different religions; but all enlightened men are now agreed that there is only one God, the Creator, Preserver, and Governor of the Universe. The Brotherhood of Man is similarly acknowledged.

Since God is one and all men are alike His children, it is reasonable to suppose that He has given only one religion. A *national* religion shows that it is not the *true* religion.

The most enlightened countries in Europe and America accepted a religion first made known to them by Asiatics, and did not reject it from false patriotism, saying "We must have national religions."

An Indian poet says : " The disease born with you, will destroy you : the medicine from a far-off mountain not born with you, will cure that disease."

Of all false patriotisms that is the worst which seeks by sophistry to defend erroneous beliefs because they are national. It promotes hypocrisy and disregard of truth among its advocates, while it is a grievous wrong to their ignorant countrymen, tending to perpetuate the reign of superstition.

Need of Prayer.

The confession has been quoted : " The Founders of the Theosophical Society do not pray." In opposition to this, the reader is strongly urged to seek Divine guidance.

The following short prayers for light may be fitly offered :

" Show me Thy ways, O Lord ; teach me Thy paths ; lead me in Thy truth and teach me ; for Thou art the God of my salvation."

"Cause me to know the way wherein I should walk; for I lift my soul to Thee."

O all-wise, all-merciful God and Father, pour the bright beams of Thy light into my soul, and guide me into Thy eternal truth.

The following prayer for spiritual light is attributed to Augustine, one of the most distinguished early Christians, born in Africa, 354 A. D.

O Lord, who art the Light, the Way, the Truth, the Life; in whom there is no darkness, error, vanity, nor death; the light, without which there is darkness; the way, without which there is wandering; the truth, without which there is error; the life, without which there is death; say, Lord, 'Let there be light,' and I shall see light and eschew darkness; I shall see the way, and avoid wandering; I shall see the truth, and shun error; I shall see life and escape death. Illuminate, O illuminate my blind soul, which sitteth in darkness and the shadow of death; and direct my feet in the way of peace.

If we make use of the light we possess, more will be given; if we act contrary to it, the light is gradually extinguished.

A man who indulges in vice of any kind cannot expect to arrive at the truth. Of the successful searcher Tennyson says:

"Perplext in faith, but pure in deeds,
At last he beats his music out."

The following prayer which Jesus Christ taught His disciples may be used daily:

"Our Father which art in heaven, Hallowed be Thy name. Thy Kingdom come. Thy will be done in earth as it is in heaven. Give us this day our daily bread. And forgive us our debts as we forgive our debtors. And lead us not into temptation, but deliver us from evil. For Thine is the kingdom, and the power, and the glory, for ever. Amen."

It has been shown that there was a time when the ancestors of the Hindus, Persians, English, French, Germans, and others, were living together in Central Asia, worshipping the same God under the self-same name—Heaven Father. May the time soon come when both Eastern and Western Aryans will kneel at the same throne of grace, and offer the same grand old prayer!

FATHER, LEAD ON!

My Father God, lead on!
Calmly I follow where Thy guiding hand
Directs my steps. I would not trembling stand,
   Though all before the way
   Is dark as night. I stay
   My soul on Thee, and say:
Father, I trust Thy love; lead on.

Thou givest strength : lead on !
I cannot sink while Thy right hand upholds,
Nor comfort lack while Thy kind arm enfolds.
    Through all my soul I feel
    A healing influence steal,
    While at Thy feet I kneel,
Father, in lowly trust : lead on.

'T will soon be o'er ; lead on !
Left all behind, earth's heart-aches then shall seem
E'en as the memories of a vanished dream ;
    And when of griefs and tears
    The golden fruit appears,
    Around the eternal years,
Father, all thanks be Thine ! Lead on !

RAY PALMER.

www.ingramcontent.com/pod-product-compliance
Lightning Source LLC
Chambersburg PA
CBHW020306090426
42735CB00009B/1244